About the book and the author:

Originally from Germany, Janik lived in the UK for six years. He moved there for a six-month internship, which turned into a more than six-year-long stay in the country. A step that was driven by a very open welcome, which then transformed into a profound love for the country and its people. Despite initial challenges in adapting to British sarcasm and culture, Janik quickly grew to appreciate the nation's unique charm. What captivated him most was the openness and humour of the British—a quality they often underplay themselves. From the breathtaking countryside to the vibrant and diverse culture, the UK became more than a destination; it became a second home.

Janik Erhart

A Foreigner's Guide to British Humour

Publisher's note

This book explores the unique and often complex world of English humour, renowned for its sarcasm, sharp observations and sometimes a lack of limits. As humour is inherently subjective, readers may encounter jokes, anecdotes, or references that feel provocative or challenging. Some content may reflect historical or cultural attitudes that differ from contemporary values.

The author wishes to emphasise that the intention is never to offend or alienate anyone. However, it is important to acknowledge that a certain degree of irreverence and offensiveness is an intrinsic part of British humour. Its charm lies in its ability to poke fun at societal norms, explore uncomfortable truths, and occasionally tread on sensitive ground - all in the spirit of provoking thought and laughter.

The author encourages readers to approach this work with an open mind, appreciating the cultural context in which English humour thrives. May this book bring you joy, laughter, and insight into one of the most distinctive comedic traditions in the world.

First version: December 2024

The automated analysis of the work in order to obtain information, in particular about patterns, trends and correlations in accordance with Section 44b UrhG ("Text und Data Mining") is prohibited.

© Janis Eckart 2024, Kalifenweg 7, 70567 Stuttgart

This work is protected by copyright.

ISBN:

Paperback 9798301966613

Independently published

"British humour is very cruel. I love it. It's my favourite kind of humour; if it isn't cruel and funny it doesn't really cut the cake for me."
Elton John

"What is so special about the British sense of humour? Perhaps it's the ability to laugh at ourselves. That has been one of our great strengths as a people, and it's something we can share with the world."
Possibly Queen Elizabeth II

"Let us not take ourselves too seriously. None of us has a monopoly on wisdom."
Definitely Queen Elizabeth II

For a world with more laughter.

Content

Part 1: The introduction to British humour.................8

  Why would a German write a book about British humour?... 8

  The history of British humour 10

    Medieval roots..................................... 13

    Shakespeare.. 18

    The 18th century 19

    The rise of music halls......................... 21

    Technological advancements 24

  So what is British humour nowadays? 30

    The wider toolkit of British humour 37

    Movies with distinct British humour 46

Part 2: Practice 49

  Wordplay 49

    Puns – Double Entendre..50

    Puns - Homophones 75

  Situational jokes..89

  Knock-knock jokes... 128

  Riddles.. 136

Part 1: The introduction to British humour

Welcome to this book of British humour, where you will find humour, which is witty, subtle, sarcastic and sometimes absurd. British Humour is often based on the contrast between what is said and what is meant or the absurdity of everyday life. Some claim it does not exist, some think it is the essence of life, so let us explore this concept of British humour.

Why would a German write a book about British humour?

You may wonder why an author with German heritage would write a book about British humour. It is down to a personal connection to the British Islands and their culture. Having grown up in Germany and having lived in Britain for six years, I have learned to appreciate the British sense of humour and its diversity. British humour can be used in everyday situations, no matter how bad they seem. In the United Kingdom, no situation is too serious for a good joke. A world that seems to turn more and more crazy by the day, needs this kind of humour, this kind of light-heartedness. Therefore, this book will try to share insights into the history of British humour, how it evolved over time and then share a variety of everyday jokes. I have selected jokes that I think are funny, clever and representative of British humour. There are some explanations and cultural references to help you understand the jokes better. I hope you will enjoy reading this book and laugh along.

But before you start, a word of warning is needed: British humour is not for the faint-hearted. It can be rude, offensive and controversial. It can poke fun at anyone and anything, including politics, religion, nationality, sexuality and even the sacred royal family. So, if you are easily offended, you may want to skip some jokes or put the book down altogether. But if you are open-minded and curious, you may discover a new way of looking at the world and laughing at it as well as yourself.

So, are you ready to dive into the world of British humour? Then let's begin with a classic joke:

"How many Germans does it take to change a light bulb?" - "One. They are efficient and don't have any sense of humour."

The history of British humour

The history of British humour is a journey that travels through centuries, reflecting the dynamic interplay of cultural, societal and historical influences. From its roots in medieval literature to its contemporary global presence, British humour has evolved, adapted and left an indelible mark on the comedic landscape. We will look at the history of British humour before diving into the different styles and jokes Britain has to offer.

Figure 1: The different countries of the United Kingdom: Wales, Northern Ireland, Scotland and England

The origins of British humour are complex and challenging to pinpoint. This is down to a rich variance of influences from the different countries of Britain and significant contributions from overseas. British humour is a dynamic and ever-evolving cultural phenomenon that has been shaped by historical, social and global factors. One of the challenges in tracing the roots of British humour lies in the multifaceted nature of the country itself. The United Kingdom comprises four distinct countries – England, Scotland, Wales and Northern Ireland – each with its own unique cultural traditions, dialects and historical experiences. These regional variations contribute to a diverse comedic landscape, making it difficult to attribute British humour to a singular source. However, the sense of humour in all those countries have sarcasm, self-depreciation and the humour about everyday life in common. A joke like the following can be heard all over the islands, potentially even in Scotland:

"An Irishman, an Englishman and a Scotsman watch their dead friend pass by. "Oh and I owed him £100", says the Irishman, putting the money on top of the coffin. "So did I", says the Englishman, doing the same. "Me too", says the Scotsman, writing out a cheque for £300 and taking the change."

The joke we just heard, is referring to the stereotype of Scottish people being a little bit thrifty with money. Political and social factors have influenced British humour over the centuries. The country's long and storied history, marked by periods of monarchy, imperialism, war and social change, has provided a rich source of comedic material.

Furthermore, British humour has been shaped by interactions with other cultures. The British Empire, at its "zenith" spanned the globe, bringing diverse influences and perspectives to the forefront of the nation's consciousness. This intercultural exchange has left a mark on British comedy, with elements of humour drawing from a global pool of traditions. Therefore, it is difficult to define British humour as purely British, one could even say that what is referred to as British humour is actually a very global humour, with influences from many corners of the planet.

One of the defining features of British humour is its reliance on self-depreciation, political touch and understatement. Instead of relying on overt punchlines, British comedians and writers often use clever language and a dry delivery to elicit laughter. This preference for the nuanced and the absurd can be traced back to the traditions of British literature, where authors like Oscar Wilde and P.G. Wodehouse mastered the art of wit and satire, challenging the status quo of society. The tradition of British sketch comedy, through shows like "Monty Python's Flying Circus" or "Spitting Image" has also played a pivotal role in shaping the country's comedic identity. These sketches often feature absurd scenarios, surreal humour and a disregard for conventional comedic structures, influencing generations of comedians both in the UK and abroad. The advent of mass media in the last decades, including television, the internet and social media, has further accelerated the exchange of comedic ideas across borders. British shows, like "Mr. Bean" have become a global export, with comedians, sitcoms and sketches gaining international acclaim and influencing humour worldwide. How did British humour become so famous and where does it come from? The following will guide you through the history and try to answer these questions.

Medieval roots

The roots of British humour can be traced back to the role of jesters and minstrels, who entertained the royal courts and the people with their witty and often cheeky performances. These performers used various techniques to make their audiences laugh, such as mockery, satire, slapstick, wordplay and absurdity, the key styles of British humour today. They also challenged the social norms and authority figures of their time, poking fun at kings, priests and peasants alike. Some of the earliest documented examples of British humour are found in plays of the 15th century and make fun of the social powers of the era. Here are some of the plays that were preserved over the last centuries:

The "**Satire of the Three Estates**" is a late mediaeval Scottish morality play written by Sir David Lyndsay. It premiered in 1552 in public and was printed in 1602, which allowed the story to be passed along over the centuries. Lyndsay was a Scottish poet and diplomat born in the early 16th century. He is best known for his works that satirised the social and political issues of his time. The "Satire of the Three Estates" is considered one of the most important works of Scottish literature, during that time. It is a satirical piece that criticises the corruption and abuses of power within the three traditional estates of mediaeval society: The first estate reflected the clergy, the second estate consisted of the nobility and the third estate included the common people or peasants. The satire highlights the hypocrisy, moral decay and injustices within each estate. The main character serves as a mouthpiece for the author's views and embarks on a journey through the "Kingdom of Unity". During his journey, he encounters representatives of each estate, including the corrupt and greedy church officials, the immoral and oppressive nobility and the oppressed common folk. Through various episodes and dialogues, Lyndsay exposes the vices and shortcomings of each estate. The play uses humour, allegory and sharp wit to convey its criticisms. Satire was a popular literary form during this period and it provided a way for writers to comment on the social and political issues of the time while entertaining their audience.

The **"Debate of the Horse, Goose and Sheep"** is a medieval literary work that belongs to the genre of "debate poetry" and is thought to have been written in the 15th century, by John Lydgate. This type of poetry typically features metaphorical animals engaged in a debate, discussing various aspects of human morality. In the poem, the horse, the goose and the sheep engage in a lively and often humorous debate about their usefulness to men, with a lion and an eagle being the jury[1]. Each animal pre-

---

[1] The Ecology of Late Medieval Warfare in Lydgate's "Debate of the Horse, Goose, and Sheep"; Jeremy, Withers, 2011

sents its case, arguing for its own importance and superiority over the others, all of them with a focus on their military use. The horse asserts to be a symbol of strength and nobility and argues for its value in warfare and chivalry, emphasizing its role in battles and tournaments. The goose, often associated with foolishness and naivety, presents a case for its feathers to be a basis for arrows and therefore essential for warfare. The sheep argues for its usefulness in providing wool for clothing, which is needed during war and peace. The dialogue is full of irony and sarcasm, such as when the goose says: "I am the best singer in the world. My voice is sweet and clear. I can make any melody that pleases the ear." A statement that is clearly contradicted by reality. "The Debate of the Horse, Goose and Sheep", like many works from the medieval period, reflects the cultural and intellectual climate of its time. The poem has several underlying messages. It shows the dependency of warfare on animals as sinews were used for bows, feathers for the arrow-shafts and horses for combat and moving supplies. The poem highlights that animals are better off without humans, who solely use them for a purpose. The question might be asked, on who is superior in the animal-human relationship, with humans depending on the force and products of animals, and animals being able to live independently. Furthermore, the poem questions the purpose of warfare at the time and may shine a light on the critical view of Lydgate regarding the purpose and effects of war. With the animals debating in front of a juridical system, it shows that Lydgate emphasises the necessity and capability of the legal system, to avoid warfare and therefore the slaughter of human and animals. The poem combines elements of satire and animal fable to engage with social and moral issues, offering both entertainment and a means of conveying deeper philosophical and ethical messages.

"The Play of the Weather" is a morality play written by the English playwriter and poet John Heywood, during the 16th century. Heywood crafted this play in the style of a morality play, a genre popular in medieval and early Tudor England. The play unfolds in a fictional kingdom ruled by Jupiter, the Roman god-king. Jupiter descends to earth to understand the views of Englishmen on the weather and its ideal state. While the play is entertaining and humorous, it also serves as a vehicle for social and political commentary. The characters' arguments mirror the socio-political climate of the time, offering insights into the challenges of political leadership and the unpredictability of governance. The initial character to step onto the stage is the gentleman, seeking fair and temperate weather for his hunting expeditions. Following him is the merchant, fervently requesting fair weather accompanied by gusts to propel his ships through the seas. The ranger, desiring windier conditions, aims to boost his income by selling fallen branches. The water-miller advocates for rain to power his mill and in contrast, the wind-miller argues for wind, without rain, to fuel his own. A heated debate unfolds between the two millers, each asserting the superior utility of their respective mills. The stage then welcomes female characters – the gentlewoman, advocating for no weather to preserve her beauty when leaving the house. The laundress, reliant on the sun's heat to dry her clothes. Like the millers, their debate centres on who is more deserving – a beautiful woman or an industrious one, showing an ongoing debate at the time. Lastly, a young boy enters, yearning for wintry weather to trap birds and engage in snowball fights with his friends. The diverse characters' pleas for their preferred weather conditions create a lively and dynamic stage filled with contrasting desires and comedic interactions. As diverse needs and conflicting requests unfold, Jupiter, after careful consideration, concludes that no single member of society holds greater importance than another. Acknowledging the necessity for each individual to have some portion of their desired weather for their pursuits and occupations, he declares that the current weather conditions will persist unchanged, ensuring that everyone can find contentment, at least some of the time. The divine verdict reflects a harmonious balance that accommodates the varied needs of his earthly subjects. John Heywood's linguistic skills and wordplay are evident throughout the play with characters engaging in lively debates using a combination of prose and verse. The play reflects the fascination with classical mythology and demonstrates the continued popularity of morality plays in the 16th century.

Shakespeare

One of the most important writers from the medieval times, or some would argue from the early modern period, is William Shakespeare. He is one of the most famous poets and playwriters from the British islands and is famous worldwide. His influence in the 16th and 17th centuries significantly shaped the trajectory of British humour. His comedic genius not only entertained but also contributed to the refinement of humour as an art form. William Shakespeare, often regarded as the greatest playwriter of the English literature world, stands as a towering figure whose influence extends far beyond the realms of tragedy and romance. One aspect of his enduring legacy is his profound impact on British humour. Through his masterful command of language, ingenious wordplay and observations of human nature, Shakespeare not only entertained Elizabethan audiences but laid the groundwork for the distinctive wit and comedic sensibility that characterise British humour to this day. Shakespeare's comedic works, such as "A Midsummer Night's Dream", "Twelfth Night", and "As You Like It", are examples of his ability to intertwine humour with deep plots and multidimensional characters. These plays often feature elements like mistaken identities, love triangles and clever wordplay, providing a template for the comedic storytelling that would become a hallmark of British humour. Central to Shakespeare's influence on British humour is his unparalleled mastery of language. His use of puns, double entendres and clever repartees demonstrated the power of words as instruments of humour. Comedic devices like puns became not only a source of amusement but also a means of exploring the nuances of human communication. Shakespeare's keen observations of human nature, reflected in his comedic characters, added depth to the humour in his works. Beyond his overtly comedic works, Shakespeare's influence can be traced in the satirical elements present in many of his plays. The biting social commentary embedded in works like "Measure for Measure", which focuses on justice, corruption and purity and "The Taming of the Shrew", which is about gender politics, set a precedent for the use of humour as a tool for critique on society. This satirical tradition, evident in later British comedic literature and performances, demonstrates the enduring relevance of Shakespearean wit in addressing societal norms and injustices. The adaptability of his themes and characters has allowed subsequent generations of writers, playwriters and comedians to draw inspiration from his work. Whether it's a modern adaptation of a Shakespearean play or a contemporary sitcom incorporating elements of his humour, his legacy continues.

The 18th century

The 18th century saw the rise of satirical literature and magazines, which became important platforms for British humour. Regular magazines like "The Spectator" and "The Tatler" started to feature humorous essays and social commentaries, allowing more universal access, at least for the literate part of the population. This era marked a turning point in the democratisation of humour and politics, as literary works became more accessible to a broader audience. Satire emerged as a powerful tool for social criticism and commentary, while periodicals became a popular medium for disseminating ideas and engaging with the public. Satire was used to expose and critique societal ills, political corruption and hypocrisy. Satirists employed various techniques, including irony, sarcasm, exaggeration and caricature, to expose the wrongdoing and immorality of their targets. Notable satirists of the time included Jonathan Swift, Alexander Pope and Laurence Sterne. Swift's "Gulliver's Travels" is a satirical masterpiece that lampoons human nature, political systems and scientific entitlement. Swift is using the various societies that Gulliver is visiting to satirize human nature and the political and religious corruption of his society, which he experienced during his career in politics. Pope's poem "The Rape of the Lock" satirizes the trivialities of upper-class society. He uses the trivial events of the main character Belinda's day to satirise the superficiality and vanity of upper-class society in contemporary Britain. Sterne's "Tristram Shandy" is a satirical, picaresque novel that tells the story of Tristram Shandy's life, from his conception to his adulthood. The novel is known for its unconventional structure and its use of digressions, which are often humorous and philosophical. The novel was highly influential and is praised for its innovation and its unique style.

Periodicals, also known as magazines and journals, emerged as a prominent form of media in the 18th century. They provided an affordable platform for disseminating news, opinion and literature to a wider audience.

Periodicals like The Tatler, The Spectator and The Rambler became influential voices in British society, engaging with political and social issues and shaping public discourse and opinion. Some parts of the periodicals were often written in a witty and engaging style, using satire and social commentary for contemporary political and social critique and therefore addressing serious issues in an entertaining manner. They covered a wide range of topics, including literature, philosophy, politics, fashion and social trends. Periodicals were vital for political discourse, especially in a time when freedom of speech was often constrained by government censorship. Writers used these platforms to critique government policies, political figures and societal issues. Furthermore, periodicals were not just for entertainment or critique; they were also a medium through which intellectual debates could be conducted. For example, *The Gentleman's Magazine* (1731-1922) was collecting essays, articles and letters from various contributors, offering a written debate. It covered a wide range of topics, including politics, literature and science, reflecting the intellectual currents of the time.

The rise of music halls

As the 19th century unfolded, the Victorian era witnessed a new chapter in the evolution of British humour with music halls rising in popularity. These venues became melting pots for a diverse range of performances: music, magic, acrobatics and comedy performances. The halls offered affordable entertainment and were a popular choice for working-class people who could not afford to go to the theatre or other more expensive forms of entertainment.

Music halls became cultural hubs where humour bridged societal divides. They were large, often ornate buildings that were typically located in working-class neighbourhoods, decorated with mirrors, chandeliers and other eye-catching features. The atmosphere inside was electric and exciting. The audience was often engaged and they would often sing along to the music and join in with the jokes. People could go there to escape the harsh realities of their day to day lives and enjoy a night of entertainment. The first music halls emerged in the 1840s and the form of entertainment reached its peak of popularity in the 1890s. There were over 300 music halls only in London at the time, which were attended by hundreds of thousands of people every week. Music halls were a major force in popular culture and they played an important role in the development of British music, comedy and society in general.

Music halls featured a wide variety of acts, including:

- **Singers**: Music halls were a breeding ground for new singers and many famous performers, such as Marie Lloyd and Harry Champion got their start in music halls.
- **Comedians**: The stage of the music halls was often taken by comedians. They used a variety of styles to entertain their audiences. Some comedians were witty and sarcastic, while others were slapstick and physical.

- **Vaudeville Acts**: A mix of different performances was shown on the stages, such as magic tricks, acrobatics, juggling and pantomime performers.
- **Dancers**: Music halls also featured a variety of dancers, including ballet dancers and clog dancers.

Music halls declined in popularity in the early 20th century as cinema and other forms of entertainment became more popular. However, they left a lasting legacy on British culture.

The humour of music halls was characterised by its:

- **Working-class roots**: Music halls emerged from working-class communities and their humour often reflected the concerns and experiences of ordinary people.
- **Social commentary**: Music hall comedians frequently used humour to critique social norms, expose hypocrisy and comment on the challenges faced by everyday people.
- **Satire and parody**: Satire and parody were common tools for music hall comedians who often poked fun at authority figures, politicians and social institutions.
- **Physical humour**: Slapstick and physical comedy were also popular elements of music hall entertainment, providing light-hearted and often cheeky humour.
- **Audience participation**: Music hall performances often involved audience participation, allowing the audience to engage with the performers and add to the comedic atmosphere.

Music halls contributed to the development of several defining features of British humour, including:

- **Self-deprecating humour**: A tendency to poke fun at oneself and one's own foibles is a common element in British humour and music halls played a part in popularising this style.
- **Anti-establishment humour**: A willingness to challenge authority and question social norms is also a hallmark of British humour and music halls often provided a platform for this type of commentary.
- **Black humour and satire**: A dark and often cynical sense of humour, often used to address serious social issues, is another characteristic which music halls helped to establish.

Technological advancements

The 20th century brought big shifts in the landscape of British humour, due to political change and technological advancement. This was reflecting the changing social, cultural and political landscapes of the era. From the wordplay of the Edwardian era to the absurdist humour of Monty Python, British humour has evolved and adapted, while retaining its distinctive characteristics.

The Edwardian era, spanning from 1901 to 1914, was a period of relative prosperity and social stability in Britain. British humour during this era reflected this mood, characterised by wit, wordplay and a sense of playfulness. Authors such as P.G. Wodehouse, one of the most read humourists of the 20th century, produced novels and short stories that poked fun at social conventions and human foibles. For example, his series of Bertie Wooster and his valet Jeeves is a light-hearted series that explores the absurdities and oddities of British upper-class society in the early to mid-20th century.

The interwar period, between the two world wars, brought about economic hardship and political upheaval. British humour during this era took on a more satirical and socially conscious tone, addressing the tough challenges faced by society. Authors such as Evelyn Waugh and George Orwell used humour to critique social injustices and expose the follies of authority figures. Evelyn Waugh's works, such as "Brideshead Revisited" and "Decline and Fall" satirise the manners and conventions of the British upper class, showcasing a sharp and often dark sense of humour. He provided insightful social commentary on the changing British society, exploring themes of decline and disillusionment. George Orwell is best known for his works like "1984" and "Animal Farm" which are not typically associated with British humour in the same way as comedic writers like P.G. Wodehouse or Evelyn Waugh. Orwell's writing, especially his most famous works, tends to focus on social and political commentary, often with a dystopian edge. However, Orwell did have a role in British literature that included elements of satire and humour, albeit often in a darker fashion. In his comic novels in the 1930s "Keep the Aspidistra Flying" and "Coming up for Air" he demonstrates his anti-totalitarianism through satiric work, criticising the path the world is taking, which finally led to the Second

World War. Orwell demonstrates a keen observational humour, often mixed with a sense of irony. His humour is frequently used as a tool to criticise societal and political issues. Orwell's contribution to British humour lies in his ability to use wit and satire to shed light on the absurdities of political ideologies, propaganda and the misuse of language. It's important to note that Orwell's overall reputation and impact stem more from his role as a social and political critic rather than as a purveyor of traditional British humour. His works are influential for their analysis of power, authoritarianism and the dangers of unchecked political ideologies.

The advent of radio and television provided new platforms for creative expression and allowed broader access to news, music and humour. "The Goon Show", a radio comedy in the 1950s featuring Spike Milligan, Peter Sellers and Harry Secombe, marked a ground-breaking transition in comedic storytelling. Every aspect of contemporary life in 1950s Britain was parodied, from politics to literature to the military to education and class structure. The show stood out with surreal humour, unexpected puns and ridiculous sound effects which were used by other shows for many years to come. Michael Palin, a member of "Monty Python" described the Goons as hugely influential and praised their sense of the ridiculous, their willingness to break the rules, their love of sound effects and their ability to create whole worlds out of nothing. The documentary "The Life of Python" (1999) comments about "The Goon Show's" impact on the globally famous comedy troupe. Both shows shared a love of surreal humour, absurdist situations and nonsensical wordplay. They also both employed a wide variety of sound effects and musical numbers to create a distinctive and immersive audio experience.

The 1960s and 1970s heralded the golden era of British sketch comedy in British television with "Monty Python's Flying Circus". The crew broke conventional comedic norms and consisted of Graham Chapman, John Cleese, Terry Gilliam, Eric Idle, Terry Jones and Michael Palin. The group broke away from traditional sketch comedy formats, introducing a surreal and absurdist style that challenged conventions. Their humour, characterised by absurdity and surrealism, often took unexpected and bizarre turns, captivating a broad audience. Despite the silliness, Monty Python's sketches featured sharp social and political satire, criticizing various aspects of British society and contemporary issues. Notably, the troupe embraced cross-dressing, with male members frequently portraying female characters. Monty Python created iconic catchphrases and moments, such as "It's just a flesh wound" and the "Dead Parrot Sketch" which became embedded in popular culture. Their influence extended beyond television, as Monty Python members collaborated on successful cinema movies like "Monty Python and the Holy Grail" and "Monty Python's Life of Brian". The group's innovative approach to comedy left a mark, inspiring subsequent generations of comedians and writers worldwide. Monty Python's Flying Circus remains a cultural touchstone, celebrated for its irreverence, ground-breaking style and enduring contributions to the comedic landscape.

Social commentary continues to be the key element of humoristic shows as exemplary the satire show "Spitting Image" proved. The show was a British satirical puppet show that aired from 1984 to 1996, with a brief revival in 2020. The show used puppetry to create exaggerated caricatures of prominent figures in politics, entertainment and popular culture. At its peak, the show was watched by 15 million people. Renowned for its sharp political satire, "Spitting Image" humorously tackled current events, political decisions and scandals, providing a unique perspective on British and global affairs. "Spitting Image" gained international recognition for its unique brand of humour. The show remains a landmark in British television history for its fearless approach to satirizing the powerful and famous.

The late 20th century saw a further diversification of British humour, with the rise of stand-up comedy and the emergence of comedians from different ethnic and cultural backgrounds. Standup Comedy can be seen as an evolvement from music hall comedy and really evolved in the 70s and 80s through the "alternative comedy" movement. The movement wanted to offer an alternative to the established humour that often evolved around racism and sexism. Alternative comedy was characterized by a more politically conscious and socially aware style, often incorporating surrealism, satire and absurdity. It found a home in venues like "The Comedy Store" in London, which opened in 1979 and became a hub for new talent. Comedians like Ben Elton, Alexei Sayle and Rik Mayall emerged from this scene, bringing a fresh and rebellious energy to British comedy. Their humour was often abrasive, challenging and reflective of the changing cultural landscape of Britain, particularly in relation to politics and social norms.

By the late 1980s and 1990s, stand-up comedy had become a mainstream form of entertainment in Britain. Comedians like Eddie Izzard, Jo Brand and Billy Connolly (though Scottish, his influence was significant across Britain) became household names, performing in large venues and on television. The humour became more diverse, with comedians exploring a wider range of topics and styles, from observational humour to more experimental and narrative forms. Television shows like "Live at the Apollo" further popularized stand-up, introducing a broader audience to both established and up-and-coming comedians until today. Exemplary Henning Wehn, a German-British comedian, appeared in the show. Wehn is famous for his unique perspective on British culture as a German living in the UK. His shows often revolve around his experiences as a German living in the UK, cultural differences and humorous observations about everyday life. He refers to himself as the "German Comedy Ambassador to the UK". With his deadpan delivery style added to the humour of his performances, he is proving that there is some humour in Germans.

So what is British humour nowadays?

British comedians have achieved international success, breaking down cultural barriers. Figures like Rowan Atkinson, known for his iconic character "Mr. Bean" and Ricky Gervais, creator of "The Office" have become global comedic ambassadors. Social media and online platforms have provided new avenues for comedians to connect with audiences and experiment with comedic formats. The adaptability of British humour to new forms and mediums, coupled with its enduring core of wit, satire and irony, has ensured its lasting popularity and influence on the global stage.

But what are the pillars of British humour? George Mikes[2] stated the three characteristics that define it. The **combination of laughing at yourself, understatement and cruelty makes** the British humour unique and it's not only the existence of the three, but also the combination of the three traits that make British humour so unique and special. Therefore, let us look at the three aspects in more detail:

Laughing at oneself or self-deprecating humour, is a cornerstone of British comedy. Jokes like "Feel free to use me as a bad example. That way, I won't be totally useless." Or "I'm quite smart and intelligent. Most of the time, I don't even understand a single word of what I'm talking about." It's a style where individuals, whether comedians or everyday people, make themselves the cen-

---

[2] English Humour for Beginners; George Mikes; 1980

tre of the joke, highlighting their own flaws, mistakes or misfortunes in a way that is both humorous and humble. This approach reflects a cultural attitude that values modesty and downplays arrogance, allowing people to connect with others by showing they don't take themselves too seriously.

Furthermore, laughing about oneself shows that one can reflect upon one's own misfortune and doing, it allows an outside perspective on oneself. A perspective that is today more important than ever. Nevertheless, self-deprecating humour can also be a form of arrogance. By making a joke about oneself, one is acknowledging and laughing at one's own shortcomings, which may be subtly signalling that one is so secure in oneself that one can afford a joke about oneself. Or it can be a form of false modesty, by downplaying one's achievements, knowing that others will contradict them, thereby fishing for compliments or reassurance. While these points illustrate how self-deprecating humour can be perceived as a form of arrogance, it's important to recognize that it often genuinely reflects humility and self-awareness. The context, delivery and intent behind the joke are key to understanding whether it comes from a place of modesty or concealed arrogance. Many people use self-deprecating humour to acknowledge their flaws and show that they don't take themselves too seriously. This can foster connection and empathy, as it makes them more relatable and approachable. In many cultures, including British culture, self-deprecating humour is a way to build rapport and signal that one is not arrogant or self-important. It can serve as a social equalizer, reducing perceived differences in status or ability. Self-deprecating humour is a way for British comedians and the British public to navigate the complexities of social interaction, maintain a sense of humility and foster connection with others. It's a humoristic style that says, "I know my flaws and I'm not afraid to laugh at them" which can be both disarming and deeply human.

Examples of self-deprecating humour can be found in TV shows or in live comedy. Ricky Gervais in his role as David Brent in "The Office (UK)", often showcases self-deprecation. Brent's character is a mix of incompetence, delusion and desperate need for approval. Yet he remains strangely endearing because he often tries (and fails) to mask his flaws, making his attempts to seem important or likeable all the more humorous. Or Jo Brand, known for her deadpan delivery, often incorporates self-deprecating humour, particularly around topics of body image and societal expectations. She turns stereotypes on their head by embracing and mocking them, making her audience laugh at the absurdity of the expectations and at her own witty take on them. The most famous comedian using this kind of humour is probably Rowan Atkinson (Mr. Bean). The character of Mr. Bean is a classic example of self-deprecating humour. Bean's lack of social awareness, awkwardness and clumsiness are exaggerated to the point of absurdity, but because he's so unaware of his flaws, the audience can't help but laugh. His failures and mishaps are a key part of the humour.

Understatement is a daily occurrence in the British life. Situations are often downplayed on the islands, with the value of modesty being displayed. As an example, if someone gets the highest grade of the class, a classic reaction is "I did ok on that test" or if there was a big storm overnight, a classic understatement is "It looks like it rained a bit last night".

Therefore, understatement is a quintessential feature of British humour, often used to convey wit and irony in a subtle, indirect manner. This form of humour involves downplaying the significance, intensity or severity of a situation, usually to create a comedic effect. The understated approach is the opposite of exaggeration; instead of emphasizing something, it minimizes it, often leading to a dry, deadpan delivery that is a hallmark of British comedy. The humour in understatement often arises from the contrast between the situation and the description. For example, describing a disastrous event as "a bit of a bother" creates a humorous dissonance because the words don't match the reality, thereby highlighting the absurdity of the situation. One of the most famous examples of understatement in British comedy is the "Black Knight" scene from "Monty Python and the Holy Grail". After having his limbs cut off in a duel, the black knight insists "It's just a flesh wound". This massive downplaying of a clearly catastrophic injury is a classic use of understatement for comedic effect. Or Douglas Adams's writing is full of understatement. For example, in his book "The Hitchhiker's Guide to the Galaxy", the earth's destruction is described as "mostly harmless". This vast understatement, given the complete annihilation of the planet, adds to the book's absurd and comedic tone. A few further examples are the following.

Response to a challenge:

- Saying: "It's not the easiest task."
- Reality: It's like climbing Mount Everest.

Personal achievements:

- Saying: "I managed to finish a small project."
- Reality: I basically rewrote physics with that project.

Weather commentary:

- Saying: "It's a bit chilly today."
- Reality: It might as well be Antarctica.

After an accident:

- Saying: "I've had a little accident with the car."
- Reality: The car looks like it went through a war zone.

Cruelty in British humour is a notable and complex aspect that reflects the darker, more biting side of the comedic tradition in the UK. This form of humour often involves harsh or cutting jokes, often at the expense of others. In everyday life, cruel humour can be putting tape on the laser of a computer mouse of a co-worker or making someone believe something that is untrue. For the last, George Mikes is telling the story of a man that is invited to a nudist party or at least thinks so[3]. On arrival he is asked by the butler, who is one of the conspirators, to undress. When naked, he is announced and enters a room where everyone else is dressed in suits and evening gowns. The victim of such a joke needs to accept the joke with good humour, otherwise he is seen as boring, without any sense of humour. The only way of revenge is by means of an even crueller joke.

British humour frequently delves into dark and morbid themes, often making jokes about death, suffering or other grim subjects. This is seen in the tradition of black comedy, where the humour comes from the absurdity or inevitability of life's darker moments. The cruelty often lies in the detachment or coldness with which these topics are treated, providing a sharp contrast to more sentimental or comforting types of humour. Sarcasm and wit are often used in a cruel way to mock or belittle others. This type of humour can be sharp and ruthless, aiming to expose hypocrisy, stupidity or other perceived flaws in a person or system. The cruelty here is intellectual, using clever language to deliver a stinging critique. Another form of cruelty in British humour involves the public humiliation or embarrassment of characters. Shows like "Fawlty Towers" or "The Office" are built around characters who frequently find themselves in humiliating situations, often due to their own flaws or failures. The hu-

---

[3] English Humour for Beginners; George Mikes; 1980

mour lies in the audience's discomfort, as they witness the characters' suffering.

Examples can be seen in TV shows, like the "Blackadder" series, which is known for its sharp wit and often cruel humour. Characters frequently insult and demean each other in clever cutting ways. For example, Edmund Blackadder's constant belittling of his servant Baldrick is both cruel and hilarious, with Baldrick's stupidity and naivety making him an easy target for Blackadder's biting sarcasm. Even "Monty Python", known for its absurdity and surrealism, involves cruelty. The famous "Dead Parrot" sketch, for instance, involves a pet shop owner cruelly refusing to acknowledge that a clearly deceased parrot is dead, frustrating the customer to no end. The humour comes from the ridiculousness of the situation, but also from the cruelty of the shopkeeper's denial.

Cruelty in British humour serves multiple purposes: it challenges social norms, exposes human folly and often pushes the audience to confront uncomfortable truths. While it can be harsh, it's also a powerful tool for satire and social commentary, allowing comedians to address serious issues in a way that is both entertaining and thought-provoking. This darker edge is a significant part of what makes British humour distinct, giving it a depth and complexity that resonates with audiences who appreciate humour that isn't afraid to be biting or brutal.

The wider toolkit of British humour

Now that we looked at the crucial characteristics, this chapter tries to show further characteristics of British humour. Some of them overlap with each other and one could for sure argue that some aspects are missing. This is an attempt at summarising any further linguistic tools that are used in British Humour.

Irony

The understanding of irony is one of the most basic parts of British humour. It is used for satire, social commentary and to add depth and complexity to storytelling. Irony is a literary and rhetorical tool where there is a discrepancy between what is said and what is meant or between what is expected to happen and what actually occurs. It involves a contrast between appearance and reality, creating a situation where the audience or reader may find something unexpected.

There are several types of irony:

- **Verbal irony**: This occurs when a speaker says something but means the opposite. It is often used for sarcasm or to convey a point in a more impactful way. Example: Saying "What a beautiful day" during a heavy rainstorm or friends buying skydiving lessons for someone afraid of heights. And the receiving persons says "Oh, I cannot wait."
- **Situational irony**: This arises when there is a contrast between what is expected to happen and what actually happens in a situation.

Example: If a fire breaks out in a fire station and it burns down, it is ironical as the fire station is there to prevent other houses from burning down. Or saying, "It's a great time to go for a swim." during a freezing cold day in winter.

- **Dramatic irony**: This occurs when the audience or reader knows something that the characters in a narrative do not, creating tension or suspense.

    Example: In a play, the audience is aware that a character is walking into a trap, but the character is oblivious.

Sarcasm

Sarcasm is a form of verbal irony that involves saying something but meaning the opposite, aimed at a person. It is expressed through a tone of voice or with a facial expression that implies mockery. It's a way of expressing one's thoughts in a cutting or bitter manner, typically with the intent to mock, criticise or ridicule. It is mostly a covert "attack" hidden within a statement which says the opposite of what is meant, whereby sarcasm employs the stylistic device of irony. It is used a lot on the British islands, in the office, between friends and just generally in everyday life.

Key features of sarcasm include:

- **Opposite meaning**: The literal meaning of the words spoken is contrary to the intended meaning. Sarcasm relies on the audience's ability to recognize this incongruity.

Example: In a discussion saying, "Oh, you are so smart", with the tone and context indicating that they actually mean the opposite.

- **Tone and delivery**: Sarcasm is often delivered with a particular tone of voice, emphasis or facial expressions that helps convey the speaker's true sentiment. The tone is crucial in distinguishing sarcasm from a straightforward statement and avoid any misunderstanding.

  Example: If someone makes a mistake, another person might say, "Nice job", with a sarcastic tone and perhaps a raised eyebrow.

- **Intent**: Sarcasm is usually employed to criticise, mock or make a point in a humorous sharp or cutting way. It often relies on shared understanding between the speaker and the listener.

  Example: In response to a trivial complaint, someone might say, "Oh, the tragedy of your life", to sarcastically downplay the significance of the complaint.

While sarcasm can be an effective form of communication in certain contexts, it's important to be mindful of its potential to be misunderstood or to cause offence, as its success often depends heavily on the relationship and understanding between the people involved.

Satire

Satire is a form of literature, art or media that uses humour, irony, exaggeration or ridicule to criticise and mock people, institutions or societal conventions. The primary goal of satire is often to bring about change by exposing and criticising the flaws or absurdities of its target in an entertaining way. This is often used in comedy shows commenting on political life, like "Frankie Boyles's New World Order", which dissects weekly news with a satirical approach.

Key elements of satire include:

- **Exaggeration**: Satire often involves exaggerating aspects of a situation, person or institution to highlight their flaws or absurdities.
- **Parody**: Satirical works may imitate the style of a particular genre or work while using it to criticise or mock its conventions.
- **Social commentary**: Satire is a tool for social commentary, addressing issues, behaviours or attitudes in society. It aims to prompt reflection of the spectators and the people the critique is aimed at.

Satire has been a powerful tool throughout history for challenging authority, questioning societal norms and promoting critical thinking. Famous examples of satirical works include George Orwell's "Animal Farm" Jonathan Swift's "Gulliver's Travels" and the satirical cartoons of artists like Honoré Daumier. Satire can be a potent force for social and political critique, providing a lens through which people can view and question the world around them.

Banter

Banter is a form of light-hearted, playful and witty conversation characterised by teasing, joking and good-natured humour. It's a social interaction where people engage in a back-and-forth exchange of clever remarks, teasing each other without any harmful or malicious intent. Banter is typically spontaneous and it often involves quick and witty responses.

Key features of banter include:

- **Playful teasing**: Banter often involves making playful and friendly jabs or teasing comments. It's important that these remarks are meant in a good-natured way and are not intended to hurt or offend.
- **Reciprocal exchange**: Banter is a two-way street. It involves mutual participation, with both parties contributing to the playful and humorous conversation.
- **Light-hearted tone**: The tone of banter is generally light-hearted and the atmosphere is fun and enjoyable. It's not meant to be too serious or confrontational.
- **Quick-witted responses**: Banter often relies on quick thinking and witty responses. Participants engage in a friendly verbal sparring, showcasing their ability to think on their feet.
- **Social bonding**: Banter is a common form of social interaction that helps building and strengthening rela-

tionships. It fosters a sense of camaraderie and shared humour among those involved.

Banter can occur in various settings, such as among friends, family members, colleagues or even strangers in a casual environment. It's a way for people to connect, have fun and enjoy each other's company through humour and playful teasing. It's important, however, to be mindful of the context and the comfort level of all participants to ensure that the banter remains enjoyable for everyone involved. Banter can sometimes even be crossing a line, which most often is fine for the people involved. But it can be difficult to judge from the outside and could be understood as bullying or confrontational, without knowing the exact relationship between the people involved. As many parts of humour this is heavily dependent on the relationship between the people. For example, calling your friend a "maggot" or a "weirdo" is banter, but can be seen strange from an outsider perspective.

Dark humour

Dark humour and cruelty are very close to each other an part of each other. Macabre elements in British humour involve a dark, grim or morbid fascination with death, the supernatural or unsettling themes. British humour sometimes incorporates macabre elements to create a unique blend of comedy and darkness. This type of humour often finds amusement in the absurdity or grim aspects of life and death and can be a way of dealing with mortality and the absurdity of life. It is often seen in movies, but also in literature.

British film and television have produced dark comedies that explore macabre themes. A perfect example of this is director Tim Burton's series "Wednesday", about the daughter of the Addams Family. They live in a creepy mansion filled with oddities, like a family tree made of human hands and enjoy morbid activities such as spider parties. Another dark comedy sitcom that took dark humour to a new level is "The League of Gentlemen", from the 1990s. The programme is set in Royston Vasey, a fictional town in northern England, following the lives of bizarre characters of the town and deals with taboo subjects such as death, violence and social awkwardness.

Dark humour also found its way into magazines, with books like "Roger's Profanisaurus Dictionary" being well known. It was published by the magazine publisher Viz and is the extreme end of macabre humour featuring sexual obscenities and lavatorial explorations. The magazine "Magna Farta" is a good example that shows that the limits of dark humour in Britain are nearly limitless. The magazine is the result of words that the readers of Roger's Profanisaurus have sent to the authors, who collected them and printed the dictionary. A few examples from the book:

- "Wet Penny: A circular piss-stain on the trouser frontage, caused by insufficient shaking of the wang"[4]
- "Whalesong: A melodic, though, slightly eerie sequence of whines, squeaks, clicks and whistles that emanate from a toilet cubicle"[5]
- "DIPS: acronym. Paris Hilton's car wing mirrors. Drunken Impact Protection System."[6]

Also, short everyday jokes can have a macabre touch to them, which emphasises the pointe but could also lead to a joke not being everyone's taste. The following dark jokes may serve as an example:

- At my boss's funeral, I leaned down and whispered to the coffin: "Who's thinking outside the box now, Brian?"
- "I had a vasectomy because I didn't want any kids. But when I got home, they were still here."
- "I tried to warn my son about the dangers of Russian roulette. But it went in one ear and out the other."
- "My wife thinks we should allow our pets to share our bed, so I agreed. After ten minutes of flapping about, the goldfish finally settled down."

---

[4] Roger's Profanisaurus: The Magna Farta; edited by Graham Dury, Davey Jones & Simon Thorp; 2008, p. 460
[5] Roger's Profanisaurus: The Magna Farta; edited by Graham Dury, Davey Jones & Simon Thorp; 2008, p. 461
[6] Roger's Profanisaurus: The Magna Farta; edited by Graham Dury, Davey Jones & Simon Thorp; 2008, p. 121

Puns and wordplay

All the previous described characteristics rely on puns and wordplay used at the right time to deliver the jokes and humour to an audience. Puns, involving the exploitation of words with multiple meanings or similar-sounding words with different spelling and meaning, are crucial in various forms of British humour. One prominent example is the use of double entendre, where words or phrases carry dual meanings, often with a sexual or suggestive undertone. Sarcasm and irony are also integral, with comedians cleverly saying one thing while meaning the opposite, relying on the audience's recognition of the incongruity for comedic impact. Wit and clever repartee are common in British comedy, whether in stand-up or scripted performances. Comedians frequently employ wordplay, literary references and unexpected manipulations of language. Absurdity and surrealism, exemplified by shows like "Monty Python's Flying Circus" often using wordplay to create bizarre and unexpected situations. Malapropisms, the incorrect use of words similar in sound but different in meaning, add to the humour in British sitcoms and jokes. Language-based sketch comedy, as seen in shows like "A Bit of Fry & Laurie" or "The Two Ronnies", features wordplay as a central element, with characters engaging in clever linguistic exchanges.

A classic example for wordplay is the Star Wars related saying "May the fourth be with you", sounding similar to the famous movie quote: "May the force be with you". A similarity that resulted in the fourth of May being an annual day of celebration for Star Wars fans around the world.

Movies with distinct British humour

To finish the theoretical part and slowly getting ready to jump into the practical jokes, here are a few picks of classic British movies and TV series that not only made British humour legendary but are also perfect for a good laugh. They are great to get a feeling for the British sense of humour and see how it developed over the centuries.

- **"Monty Python and the Holy Grail"** (1975): One of the most beloved and influential comedies in film history. Known for its absurd humour, memorable quotes and innovative style, the movie has become a cult classic. The film is a humorous retelling of the legend of King Arthur and his knights' quest to find the Holy Grail. True to Monty Python's style, the narrative is nonlinear and filled with absurdities. The film is famous for its absurdist humour, where logic and reality are frequently disintegrated. The humour often comes from the parallelism of a medieval setting with modern references.
- **"Fawlty Towers"** (1975-1979): A sitcom starring John Cleese as the eccentric and often irritable hotel owner Basil Fawlty, which is widely regarded as one of the greatest television comedies of all times. The show is set in the fictional seaside hotel, Fawlty Towers, located in the English Riviera town of Torquay. The hotel is run by Basil Fawlty, a rude and incompetent hotelier, along with his more competent but long-suffering

wife, Sybil. Each episode revolves around the day-to-day operations of the hotel, which inevitably spiral into chaos due to Basil's incompetence, arrogance and temper. The story typically involves a series of misunderstandings and escalating situations that lead to frantic attempts by Basil to cover up mistakes, only to make things worse.

- **"Absolutely Fabulous"** (1992-2012): The show revolves around the chaotic lives of Edina "Eddy" Monsoon, a public relations professional and her best friend, Patsy Stone. Set in London, the series provides a satirical look at the world of fashion, PR, celebrity culture and the excesses of the 1990s.
- **"Four Weddings and a Funeral"** (1994): A British romantic comedy film directed by Mike Newell and written by Richard Curtis. It is one of the most beloved and successful British films of the 1990s, known for its charming blend of humour, romance and heartfelt emotion. The film became a cultural touchstone and helped to catapult its lead actor, Hugh Grant, to international stardom.
- **"Snatch"** (2000): "Snatch" is a British crime comedy film written, directed and produced by Guy Ritchie. Set in the fictional English town of Brick Lane, it tells the story of a group of small-time crooks who become entangled in a diamond heist. A strong cast, including Brad Pitt as Mickey, a traveller boxer and Jason Statham as Turkish, a box promoter, are making this humour loaded movie a must see.

- **"The Office" (UK)** (2001-2003): Created by Ricky Gervais and Stephen Merchant, this mockumentary sitcom set the stage for a new style of comedic storytelling. Set up like a documentary, it brings a dry, uncomfortable humour which is rooted in the realities of office life. The style was copied for mockumentaries like "The Office (US)" (2005) or the recent German mockumentary "Der Discounter" (since 2021).
- **"The Grand Budapest Hotel"** (2014): While the director, Wes Anderson, is American, the film has a distinctive British humour style and features a stellar British cast. The film's humour is a blend of deadpan delivery, absurd situations, visual gags and clever dialogue.
- **"Derry Girls"** (2018-2020): A sitcom set in Derry, Northern Ireland, during the 1990s, following the lives of a group of teenage girls and one English boy as they navigate adolescence within the backdrop of The Troubles.
- **"The Inbetweeners"** (2008-2010): A British teen comedy television series created by Iain Morris and Damon Beesley. It follows the lives of four sixth-form boys as they steer their way through the various trials and tribulations of growing up. Until today, this one of the most famous British comedy series, in the generation aged 25-45 years.
- **"Spitting Image"** (1984-1996 & 2020-2022): This British satirical puppet show, which aired in television, is known for its caricature puppets representing prominent public figures, like celebrities, politicians and members of the royal family.

Part 2: Practice

The whole book so far covered a lot of history, theory and references to movies, books and individuals. The rest of this book is now dedicated to jokes that should help you to understand the British language better, learn a few British jokes and just make you smile. The chapter is divided in different kind of styles of jokes and the individual jokes have a little explanation on where the humour lies within them.

The most important thing about jokes is to never forget that they are for humour and entertainment and should not be taken too seriously. Jokes can be political or socially critical, but are an important aspect of free speech, as they bring humour and therefore understanding, into difficult subjects. By doing that, they allow more lighthearted conversations about difficult subjects and bring people together.

Wordplay

Words are powerful tools, but they're also full of surprises. English is filled with words that sound alike, look alike or even mean different things depending on how they're used. When we play with these qualities, we create wordplay jokes or puns, which turn language into a playground of humour. Those jokes are the oldest form of humour, dating back to ancient times. Some of Shakespeare's most memorable lines are full of puns and famous comedians still use them today. Why? Because wordplay taps into something universal: the surprise of realizing that a single word or phrase can contain multiple meanings. Puns don't require a lot of setup or elaborate storytelling. Instead, they're simple, quick and often elicit groans or laughs as people realize they've been tricked by the double meaning. A good wordplay joke catches our brains off guard, making us stop and appreciate the clever twist in language. What makes these jokes so versatile is their appeal to people of all ages. Kids love puns because they play with language in a way that's easy to understand, adults appreciate them because they offer a clever mental twist. Plus, these jokes are perfect for lightening the mood in almost any situation. You can throw them into a conversation, add them to a text or tell them around the dinner table. Whether they're met with laughs, groans or playful eye-rolls, puns have a way of creating a sense of shared amusement.

This chapter dives into the art of wordplay, focusing on jokes that use words with double meanings, but also words that sound like other words, yet have very different meanings and spellings.

Puns – Double Entendre

The first section of the practical application of jokes will look at those jokes that are based on words (or phrases) that have more than one meaning and deliver the joke through the understanding of both meanings. One of the meanings is usually straightforward and literal, while the other is often more suggestive or figurative. These jokes are generally referred to as puns, but we differentiate between double entendre puns and homophones puns, which will be looked at in the next chapter. Let us start with an example of a double entendre pun:

"My father is a bus driver who circles Big Ben in London. He works around the clock."

The joke here is delivered through the double meaning of "work around the clock". The first meaning of the expression is that the father is always working, while the second meaning is that he is geographically working around the Big Ben, which is one of the most famous clock towers in the UK, if not the world.

Up next, you'll find a handpicked selection of jokes that play with double meanings. Each joke comes with a brief explanation, highlighting the different meanings or structures that make it funny. For clarity, the keyword or phrase in each joke will be bolded to help you spot the clever twist. Enjoy reading and see how language can turn everyday words into moments of laughter!

Joke	Explanation
Which building in London has the most **stories**? The public library.	1) "Stories" can refer to the levels or floors of a building. 2) "Stories" also refers to books or tales that people read.
I just found out my toaster was not waterproof. I was **shocked**.	1) "Shocked" refers to the feeling of surprise or disbelief, as in being startled by unexpected news. 2) It also refers to a real electric shock.
If I hit you with a duracell, I'll get charged with **battery**.	1) A "battery" is a device that stores electrical energy—like a Duracell battery. 2) In a legal sense, battery is a criminal offense that involves physically attacking someone.
My medieval servant was missing, so I tried to look him up on the internet- It said "**Page** not found".	1) In medieval times, a "page" was a young servant or attendant. 2) On the internet, "Page not found" is a common error message when a webpage is unavailable or missing.

Joke	Explanation
I had a **date** last night. It was perfect. Tomorrow I will try a grape.	1) A "date" is a social outing or romantic meeting, often implying the person had a great time. 2) A date is also a type of fruit, just like a grape.
My friend worked at the Zoo, circumcising elephants. The pay was bad but the **tips** were huge.	1) "Tips" refer to extra earnings, which can be a major part of income in certain jobs. 2) It also refers to the body part removed during circumcision.
What did the football coach do when the pitch started to flood? He sent the **subs** on.	1) In football, "subs" refers to substitute players. 2) It also refers to "submarines" as if the coach is sending them out to deal with the flooding.
Why was the computer cold? Because it left its **Windows** open!	1) Windows in the context of computers refers to the Microsoft Windows operating system. 2) Literally, leaving windows open could make a room cold by letting in outside air.

Joke	Explanation
What did the cannibal choose as his last meal? **Five Guys**.	1) Five Guys is a popular fast food restaurant known for its burgers and fries. 2) The joke suggests that the cannibal, who eats people, chose to eat five guys (as in five men).
Why don't scientists trust atoms? Because they **make up everything**.	1) "Make up everything" means that atoms are the basic building blocks that make up all matter in the universe. 2) Make up can also mean to fabricate or lie about something.
Einstein finally finished his relativity theory. It was **about time**.	1) "About time" can be used to express relief that something long-awaited has happened. 2) It also refers to the concept of time, which is central to Einstein's theory of relativity.
What do polar bears and plumbers have in common? They both want a good **seal**.	1) In the context of polar bears, a seal refers to the marine mammal that is a primary food source for polar bears. 2) In the context of plumbers, a seal refers to a watertight closure

Joke

"I have a split personality", said Hans, being **Frank**.

Explanation

1) The phrase can imply that Hans is acting "frank" (honest and direct).
2) While he's literally "being Frank" (a different person) claiming to have a split personality.

Joke

My wife and I had an argument about who needs to do the laundry. Eventually I **threw in the towel**.

Explanation

1) In a conflict or argument, "throwing in the towel" means giving up.
2) A towel can also be literally being thrown into the laundry.

Joke

My wife absolutely hates it when our next door neighbour sunbathes topless in her yard. Personally, I **am on the fence**.

Explanation

1) Being "on the fence" means being neutral about something.
2) The phrase "on the fence" can also be taken literally, implying the speaker is standing on a fence, watching.

Joke

Why was Donald Trump shot in the ear? Because he did not listen to the secret service when they shouted: **"Donald duck"**.

Explanation

1) "Donald Duck" sounds like an actual warning "Duck!", meaning "get down" or "take cover."
2) Donald Duck is a famous cartoon character.

Joke	Explanation
Why did the math book look sad? Because it had too many **problems**.	1) In everyday language, "problems" refer to difficulties that cause distress or unhappiness. 2) In mathematics, "problems" refer to exercises or questions that need to be solved.
After I was arrested, my ex put a picture of me up in her flat. But she still does not admit that she **framed** me.	1) In a legal context, to be "framed" means to be falsely accused for a crime you didn't commit often by someone else. 2) "Framed" refers to placing a picture within a frame to display it.
I used to be a baker, but I couldn't make enough **dough**.	1) In baking, "dough" refers to the mixture of flour, water and other ingredients that is prepared for baking. 2) It is also slang for money or cash.
I always wanted to become a fishermen, but it is difficult to live off the **net-income**.	1) "Net income" refers to the money earned (which is difficult to live off) 2) And to the idea of catching fish with a net.

Joke	Explanation
I had to fire the person I got to mow my lawn. **He just did not cut it**.	1) "Cut it" refers to the act of mowing or trimming the lawn. 2) "Did not cut it" is an idiom meaning that someone is not good enough.
I got a new **mouse** recently. It always squeaks when I use it for my computer.	1) A "mouse" is a small animal, which is known to squeak. 2) A "mouse" is also a device used to interact with a computer.
"I am fulfilling my long dream of visiting the Tower Bridge." "What will you do when you get there?" **"I will cross that bridge when I come to it"**	1) The expression is an idiom, meaning that someone will deal with a problem when it arises. 2) It is also interpreted literally in the context of the Tower Bridge, by walking over it.
I just figured out why Teslas are so expensive. It is because they **charge** a lot.	1) "Charge" refers to the price or cost of something. 2) "Charge" also refers to the process of charging an electric vehicle, like a Tesla.

Joke	Explanation
Why did the tomato turn red? Because it saw the **salad dressing**.	1) "Dressing" refers to a sauce or condiment that is added to a salad. 2) "Dressing" also refers to the act of putting on clothes.
Why do astronauts use Linux? Because they cannot open **Windows**.	1) "Windows" of a spacecraft should not be opened in space. 2) "Windows" also refers to the Microsoft operating system, which is one of the most used systems worldwide.
My best mates and I played a game of hide and seek. It went on for hours... Well, good friends **are hard to find**.	1) The friends are difficult to find during the game as they are good at hiding. 2) Good friends are hard to come by in life in general.
My buddy keeps asking me to blow cool air on him when he gets hot but I do not like it. **I am not a fan**.	1) Not being a fan of something, therefore not liking it. 2) A "fan" is a machine that blows air. Synonym: Ventilator.

Joke	Explanation
I broke up with my girlfriend of five years because I found out she was a communist. I should have known - there were **red flags** everywhere.	1) Physical red flags, symbolising communism. 2) Warning signs in the behaviour of another person, that should lead to questioning the longevity of a relationship.
I told my wife she was drawing her eyebrows too high. She **looked surprised**.	1) Looked in the sense of her whole appearance. With the high eyebrows the face expresses a feeling of surprise. 2) She seemed surprised about it when he told her.
Did you hear about the depressed ghost? He is **going through some things**.	1) Physically walking though stuff (as he is a ghost). 2) Working through some tough times in life.
I told my doctor that I was scared of shrinking. He said I needed to calm down and learn to be a **little patient**.	1) He needs to learn some composure / not being so stressed out. 2) A physically small person that is being treated by the doctor.

Joke	Explanation
I used to be a banker, **but I lost interest.**	1) Loosing personal engagement. 2) Financial term for revenue or income for having money in a bank.
I arrived at the restaurant early. The manager said: "Do you mind **waiting** a bit?". "No" I said. "Great" he said. " Take these drinks to table nine."	1) Staying in one place until something happens, in this case, waiting for a table. 2) Working as a waiter and serving the drinks to the customers.
A man **walks into a bar.** Ouch!	1) A "bar" is an establishment where drinks are served, setting up the scene of a typical "man walks into a bar" joke. 2) "Bar" can also refer to a metal rod, which is the punchline here.
You really should try archery while blindfolded. You **do not know what you are missing.**	1) Not being aware of how enjoyable blind archery is. 2) You literally do not know what you are missing with the arrow, as you don't see anything.

Joke

I went on a date last night with a woman I met at the zoo. It was great, she is a **keeper**.

Explanation

1) Someone worth holding on to, implying that it was a great match.
2) A zookeeper, working at the zoo.

Joke

My wife threatened to divorce me when I said I was going to give our newborn daughter a silly name. So I **called her Bluff.**

Explanation

1) A bluff is an insincere threat and calling it means to challenge someone to follow through on it.
2) It's also being used as the daughter's name in the joke.

Joke

I used to **play** piano **by ear**, but now I use my hands.

Explanation

1) It refers to a musician's ability to play music without looking at sheets, just by listening and replicating music.
2) Literally playing the piano with the ear instead of hands.

Joke

My son might not be the best roofer in the world, but **he is up there**.

Explanation

1) "Up there" can mean that someone is among the best at something.
2). It also literally refers to roofers working up on roofs.

Joke	Explanation
Why don't some couples go to the gym? Because some relationships **don't work out**.	1) It can refer to not exercising at the gym or not making any sports in general. 2) It can also mean that a relationship has no successful outcome.
Last week, I built a model of Mount Everest. My son asked: "Is it **to scale?**" - "No, it is to look at".	1) "To scale" means that something is built with accurate proportions in relation to the real thing. 2) It also means to climb. So the parent asks the son to just look at the model, not climb it.
I couldn't figure out how to put my seatbelt on. Then it **clicked**.	1) "Clicked" can mean that something suddenly made sense. 2) It also refers to the sound a seatbelt makes when it fastens properly.
I have been trying to convince my dad to get a new hearing aid. But **he just will not listen.**	1) "Not listening" can mean someone is ignoring or refusing to pay attention to what you're saying. 2). In this context, the father literally cannot hear.

Joke

I couldn't figure out why the baseball kept getting larger. Then **it hit me**.

Explanation

1) "It hit me" can mean that someone suddenly realizes something.
2) It can also refer to the baseball getting closer and literally hitting the person.

Joke

Why did the German chef refuse to be a waiter? He said he couldn't handle the stress of **waiting**.

Explanation

1) "Waiting" can mean the job of a waiter, who serves food or drinks.
2) It can also refer to the act of patience. And Germans are not famous for their patience.

Joke

Midwives deserve a lot of respect. **They really help people out**.

Explanation

1) The phrase means to support people and offering assistance.
2) Midwives quite literally help people out by assisting in childbirth.

Joke

My partner told me I had to stop acting like a flamingo. So **I had to put my foot down**.

Explanation

1) The phrase means to make a firm decision, often stopping someone else's behaviour.
2). Flamingos are famous for standing on one leg, which the joke implies the person was doing.

Joke	Explanation
My boyfriend told me I was average. He was just being **mean**.	1) In maths, "mean" refers to the average value of a set of numbers. 2) It can also refer to someone acting unkind or hurtful in their words or actions.
My wife told me I should do lunges to stay in shape. That would be **a big step forward**.	1) The phrase means making significant progress. 2) It also refers to a physical exercise, where you take a step forward and lower your body.
My family thought of me as a failure. Then I invented an invisibility cloak. **If only they could see me now**.	1) The phrase implies that the person achieved something significant. 2) An invisibility cloak would make the wearer invisible, and his family cannot see him anymore.
My wife and I are in the middle of a heated argument about which ingredient to add next to the soup. It's a real **stock exchange**.	1) The stock exchange is a marketplace where shares of companies are traded. It's often associated with intense negotiations. 2). Stock is also a flavoured quid, in cooking.

Joke
Why did the cat sit next to the computer? Because it wanted to keep an eye on the **mouse**.

Explanation
1) A mouse is a device to navigate a computer.
2) A mouse is also a small animal that cats typically hunt.

Joke
I wasn't originally going to get a brain transplant, but then I **changed my mind**.

Explanation
1) "Changed my mind" is a common phrase meaning to make a different decision.
2) A brain transplant would literally involve changing your mind.

Joke
Why did the bee get married? Because it found its **honey**.

Explanation
1) In the context of bees, honey is the sweet substance they produce.
2) "Honey" is also commonly used as a term of affection between couples.

Joke
My sister just delivered a baby. **I knew she had it in her.**

Explanation
1) The phrase often means that someone has the potential or ability to achieve something.
2) The phrase can also refer to the idea that the baby was inside her during pregnancy.

Joke	Explanation
Why don't programmers like nature? It has too many **bugs**.	1) In software development, a "bug" refers to an error in the code that causes a program to malfunction. 2) In nature, "bugs" literally refer to insects.
I know a lot of jokes in sign language and I can guarantee you **no one has ever heard them**.	1) The phrase "no one has ever heard them" normally implies that the jokes are unknown. 2) If a joke is told in sign language, it is communicated visually. Therefore, no one hears the joke.
What did the football coach do when the field started to flood? **He sent the subs on.**	1) In football "subs" is short for substitutes, referring to the players who are not in the starting lineup. 2) In the context of a flood, "subs" could also be short for submarines.
My wife wont let me get a tattoo of a grizzly on each biceps. She is infringing on my right to **bear arms**.	1) "Bear arms" is a legal phrase meaning the right to carry weapons. E.g. in the USA. 2). "Bear arms" also sounds like having bear tattoos on your arms (in this case, grizzly bears).

Joke	Explanation
I didn't realize the opening of the Lego store was so popular. People were **queuing for blocks**.	1) "Queuing for blocks" is a phrase that means people were waiting in long lines, since "blocks" refers to city blocks. 2) In the context of Lego, "blocks" refers to the toy building pieces.
What did the shark say when he ate a clownfish? This **tastes a little funny**.	1) A "funny taste" means it tastes strange or unusual. 2) A clownfish is associated with clowns, who are known for being "funny" and making people laugh.
After playing the guitar for years, I thought it is easy to learn to play the piano. But it is not an easy one to **pick up**.	1) "Pick up" can mean learning a new skill, like learning to play an instrument. 2) It can also mean the act of physically lifting something.
Why did the yoghurt go to the art exhibition? Because it was **cultured**.	1) Yogurt is made by bacteria cultures that ferment the milk. 2) In a general sense, "cultured" refers to someone who appreciates art and has refined tastes.

Joke	Explanation
Did you hear about the two people who stole a calendar? **They both got six months.**	1) A calendar covers a full year, so if two people stole it, they each get half, which is six months. 2) The sentence is also implying that they each got six months in prison.
I would tell you a pizza joke…. But it is probably **too cheesy.**	1) "Cheesy" relates to the topping of a pizza. 2) "Cheesy" is also slang for something corny, often used to describe jokes that aren't very clever.
Why did the strawberry cry? Because it **found itself in a jam**.	1) "In a jam" is an expression that means being in a difficult or troublesome situation. 2) Jam is another word for a fruit spread, which implies the strawberry got crushed and cooked.
Two artists had an art contest. It ended in a **draw.**	1) In a contest, a "draw" means a tie, where neither competitor wins. 2). "Draw" also refers to the act of creating a picture, which is what artists do.

Joke	Explanation
Why are ghosts such bad liars? Because they are easy to **see through**.	1) Someone who is "easy to see through" is a bad liar, as their dishonesty is obvious. 2) Ghosts are often depicted as transparent or see-through.
How do celebrities stay cool? They have many **fans**.	1) A fan is a device used to cool people down by moving air. 2) Fans also refer to people who admire and support celebrities.
Mom, is this **safe** to eat? No, it is to keep our money.	1) In one sense, "safe" means something is not harmful and is suitable to eat. 2) Literally it also refers to a secure storage box for money or valuables.
I tried to sue the airport for misplacing my luggage. I lost my **case**.	1) In the context of luggage, a "case" refers to a suitcase or bag. 2). In legal terms, "losing a case" means losing a lawsuit.

Joke	Explanation
I was going to tell you a joke about boxing but I forgot the **punch** line.	1) In a joke, the punch line is the part that delivers the humour. 2) In boxing, a **punch** is a main action where boxers hit each other.
Why did the egg hide? It **was a little chicken**.	1) "A little chicken" means someone who is scared, sometimes only for little reason. 2) An egg can eventually turn into a chicken.
I walked in on my girlfriend having sex with her personal trainer. Me:" Ok, this is **not working out**".	1) "Working out" refers to exercising, which is what a personal trainer typically helps with. 2) "Not working out" also means that the relationship isn't going well.
What happens when a strawberry gets run over crossing the street? **Traffic jam.**	1) A traffic jam is a congestion in traffic. 2) When a strawberry is crushed, it could turn into a jam (the fruit spread).

Joke

I saw a man standing on one leg at an ATM. Confused, I asked him what he was doing.... He said:" Just **checking my balance**".

Explanation

1) At an ATM, "checking my balance" means viewing the amount of money in one's bank account.
2) It can also mean testing physical balance, like standing on one leg.

Joke

What did one plate say to the other? **Dinner is on me.**

Explanation

1) "Dinner is on me" usually means one person is offering to pay for the meal.
2) A plate literally has dinner on it, holding the food.

Joke

A guy shows up late for work. The boss yells, **'You should've been here at 8.30!'** He replies. 'Why? What happened at 8.30?'

Explanation

1) The boss wants the employee to arrive at 8:30 at his start time.
2) The employee takes it as if something special happened at 8:30, acting clueless about being late.

Joke

Why did the doctor need a red pen at work? In case she needed to **draw blood.**

Explanation

1) In medicine, drawing blood means taking a blood sample from a patient.
2). With a red pen, "draw blood" could also mean literally drawing a picture of blood.

Joke	Explanation
Arial and Times New Roman walk into a bar. "Get out of here", shouts the bartender. "We do not serve your **type!**"	1) In everyday language, type can mean a category or kind of person. 2) In typography, type refers to fonts or typefaces, like Arial and Times New Roman.
Why shouldn't you kiss anyone on the first of January? It is only the **first date.**	1) "First date" can refer to a romantic meeting, with someone for the first time. 2) "First Date" also refers to a specific day on the calendar—January 1st.
My daughter wants a pet spider for her birthday. I went to the pet store and the owner said "that'll be $200 please." I said "$200? it'll be cheaper **getting one off the web."**	1) Getting one off the web can mean buying something from the internet, often cheaper. 2) Web also refers to a spider's web, saying he could just find a spider outside for free.
My wife asked me to **put ketchup on the shopping list.** Now I cannot read it.	1) Putting ketchup on the list normally means adding "ketchup" as an item to the list of things to buy. 2) The husband took it literally and physically put ketchup on the list.

Joke	Explanation
What washes up on small beaches? **Microwaves.**	1) On small beaches, the waves that reach the shore could be small. 2) A microwave is also an appliance used for heating food, which could wash up at shore in special cases
Why did the cyborg have to rest after his long road trip? Because he had a **hard drive.**	1) A cyborg likely has a hard drive (a computer storage device) as part of its robotic components. 2) "Hard drive" can also mean a demanding journey in a vehicle.
I'd tell you a construction pun, but **I'm still working on it.**	1) In construction, projects are often incomplete or "still being worked on." 2) The speaker implies they haven't finished coming up with a good pun yet.
I know a guy who's addicted to brake fluid, but he says **he can stop any time.**	1) Brake fluid is essential for stopping a vehicle. 2) "Stopping any time" often refers to an addiction someone could stop.

Joke

After 5 long years of studying, a student comes rushing into Einstein's office shouting:
"Sir, Sir, I finally understand your theory of Special Relativity!"
Einstein rolls his eyes, **"It's about time".**

Explanation

1) Special Relativity is a theory that focuses on time and space, explaining how they're affected by the speed of an object, especially near the speed of light. So, when Einstein says, "It's about time," he's hinting that his theory is, quite literally, about time
2) The phrase "It's about time" is a common expression meaning, "Finally!" or "It took you long enough!". Einstein uses this phrase to tease the student for taking five years to get the theory.

Joke

The wife and I took a long, leisurely drive out to the country and pulled over to fill up our car's gas tank and tires. She was surprised to see that the station had a fee to fill the tires and asked me, "Why in the world do they charge for AIR?!" I responded, **"Inflation."**

Explanation

1) "Inflation" usually refers to the rise in prices over time, meaning that goods and services become more expensive.
2) "Inflation" can also mean the act of filling something with air, like inflating a tire.

Puns - Homophones

Now that we've explored double entendre puns, with clever double meanings, it's time to dive into another type of wordplay: jokes with words that sound alike but have a different spelling, the so called homophones. These jokes rely on words or phrases that have similar sounds but different spelling and entirely different meanings, creating humour from the surprise of one word standing in for another. By playing with words that sound similar but have different meanings, we can create a type of humour that's witty and quick in the best way! The humour comes from tricking our brains with words that could mean one thing but actually mean something else.

In this chapter, words like "pear" and "pair," or "witch" and "which," are the stars of the show. These jokes are often simple, but they're full of creativity. Plus, they're perfect for any setting, easy to remember and can bring a laugh (or an eye-roll) out of almost anyone.

An example of a joke in this category is the following: "Why is it so loud on a graveyard? Because of all the **coffin**."

This joke plays on a verbal similarity between the words "coffin" and "coughing." In the context of a graveyard, "coffin" normally refers to the box in which a deceased person is buried. However, here it's used as a play on the sound-alike word "coughing," which would indeed make a graveyard loud if everyone were coughing. The humour comes from the unexpected twist of associating a quiet place with a noisy activity, all through the clever sound similarity between "coffin" and "coughing."

In each of the following jokes, the word with a sound-alike counterpart will be **highlighted**. The accompanying explanation will reveal the similar-sounding word and clarify its meaning in the joke's context, helping you catch the full twist and enjoy the humour!

Joke

What did the American football coach say to the broken vending machine? Give me my **quarterback**.

Explanation

The joke plays on "quarterback", referring both to the American football position and the coach's request for his quarter (25 cents) back from the broken vending machine.

Joke

RIP to boiling water. You will be **mist**.

Explanation

The joke plays on "you will be missed", replacing "missed" with "mist" to humorously indicate that boiling water turns into mist (steam) when it evaporates.

Joke

What does a CIA agent do when it is time for bed? He goes **undercover**.

Explanation

The joke plays on the term "undercover", which refers to secretive work done by CIA agents and uses it literally to mean going under the covers (blankets) when going to bed.

Joke

Did you hear about the **kidnapping** at the playground? They woke up.

Explanation

The joke plays on "kidnapping", which usually means abducting a child but humorously refers to kids napping at the playground, implying they just woke up instead of being taken.

Joke

What does the physicist say when he meditates? **"Ohm"**

Explanation

The joke plays on "Ohm", a unit of electrical resistance, which sounds like "Aum", a sound used in meditation, humorously linking physics with meditation.

Joke

Why do cows have hooves and not feet? Because they **lactose**.

Explanation

The joke plays on the word "lactose", a sugar found in milk, sounding like "lack toes", suggesting that cows have hooves instead of feet because they have no toes.

Joke

What did America say to Britain when it fell over? **U.K?**

Explanation

The joke plays on the abbreviation "U.K." for the United Kingdom, sounding like "you okay?" to humourously imply America is checking on Britain after it falls over.

Joke

Someone asked to name two structures that hold water. I said **"Well, damn"**

Explanation

"Well, damn" is implying that the person is not sure about the answer, but at the same time a "well" and a "dam" are both structures that hold water.

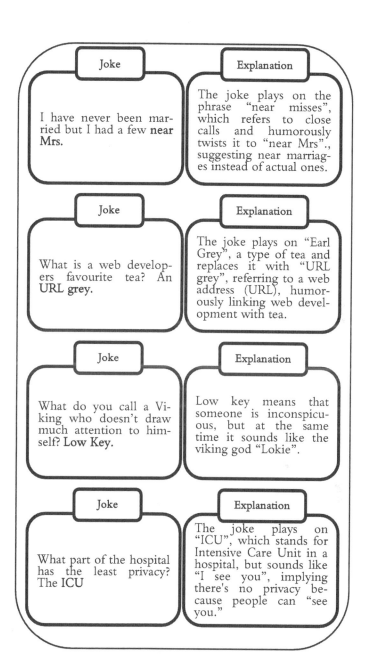

Joke

Ten plus ten and eleven plus eleven both equal the same number. Ten plus ten equals twenty and eleven plus eleven equals **twenty, too!**

Explanation

The joke plays on the phrase "twenty, too", which sounds like the number 22, while also meaning "twenty as well".

Joke

At the doctors: Can we talk about your **weight**? - Certainly, it was about 30 minutes, but the chairs were comfortable.

Explanation

The joke plays on the word "weight", which the doctor intends to mean body weight, but the patient humorously misinterprets it as "wait" time in the waiting room.

Joke

How does a penguin build its house? **Igloos** it together.

Explanation

The joke plays on "igloos", which are ice houses and sounds similar to "it glues", suggesting the penguin builds its house by glueing it together.

Joke

I ate a **kid's meal** at Mc Donalds today. His mother got really angry.

Explanation

The joke plays on the term "kid's meal", which usually means a meal intended for children, but implies the speaker ate a meal belonging to an actual kid, leading to the mother's anger.

Joke	Explanation
What happened when 50 cent went to las vegas? **51**.	The joke plays on the rapper "50 Cent", suggesting that after going to Las Vegas, he won during gambling, with 51 sounding like 50 won.
I used to work in a shoe recycling shop, but it was **sole-destroying**.	The joke plays on the word "sole", referring to the bottom part of a shoe and sounding like "soul", which implies emotional or mental distress.
What do you call a computer that sings? **A Dell**.	The joke plays on the name "Dell", referring to the computer brand, which sounds like Adele, the singer, suggesting that a computer that sings would be like Adele performing.
I got arrested for stealing kitchen utensils. It's a **whisk** I am willing to take.	The joke plays on the phrase "a risk I am willing to take", substituting "risk" with "whisk", a kitchen utensil, to create a humorous pun about stealing kitchen tools.

Joke

What do you call someone that is only kind of from Britain?
Brit-ish

Explanation

The joke plays on the word "British", splitting it into "Brit" and "ish", suggesting that the person is only partially or somewhat from Britain.

Joke

Why don't oysters donate to charity? Because they are **shellfish**.

Explanation

The joke plays on the word "shellfish", which refers to oysters and also sounds like "selfish", implying that oysters don't donate to charity because they are self-centered.

Joke

I am going to open up a sports nutrition shop. I will call it "**Whey** to go"

Explanation

The joke plays on the phrase "way to go", using "whey", a protein derived from milk used in sports nutrition, to create a pun that suggests a positive direction for the shop.

Joke

Did you hear about the cheese factory that exploded? There was nothing left but **de-brie**.

Explanation

The joke plays on "debris", meaning scattered remains and "de-brie", a pun on the cheese brie, implying that after the explosion, only cheese remnants were left.

Joke	Explanation
What part of the body always loses? **Defeat**	The joke plays on the word "defeat", which sounds like "the feet", humorously suggesting that the feet are the part of the body that always loses.
A priest, a pastor and a rabbit entered a clinic to donate blood. The nurse asked the rabbit: "What's your blood type?" "I am probably a **type O**", said the rabbit.	The joke is a play on words with "rabbit" and "rabbi", suggesting a mix-up where a rabbit mistakenly joins a priest and pastor, then guesses it's "type O" blood, as in "a typo".
The medical student asked his peer, "How did your exam on ears go today?" "It went fine. It was just an **Aural** Report."	The joke twists "oral report" into "aural report", cleverly linking the topic (ears) with a sound-alike phrase.
I cannot tell you the whole of Japanese history in one sentence but I can **samurais**.	The joke plays on "summarize", meaning to briefly explain and "samurais", the famous Japanese warriors, creating a pun that suggests summarizing Japanese history with "samurais".

Joke	Explanation
Police were called to a day care where a three-year-old was resisting **a rest**.	The joke is a pun on "resisting arrest", replacing it with "resisting a rest", meaning the child refuses to nap, creating a playful twist on legal terminology.
What is it called when you kill chickpeas? **Hum-mus-ide**.	The joke plays on "homicide", the act of killing and replaces it with "hummus-ide", a pun suggesting the "killing" of chickpeas, the main ingredient in hummus.
The numbers 19 and 20 got into a fight. **21**.	The joke plays on the number "21" sounding like "twenty won".
I tried to catch fog yesterday. **Mist**.	The joke plays on "mist", which sounds like "missed", humorously suggesting the speaker failed to catch the fog, which turned into mist.

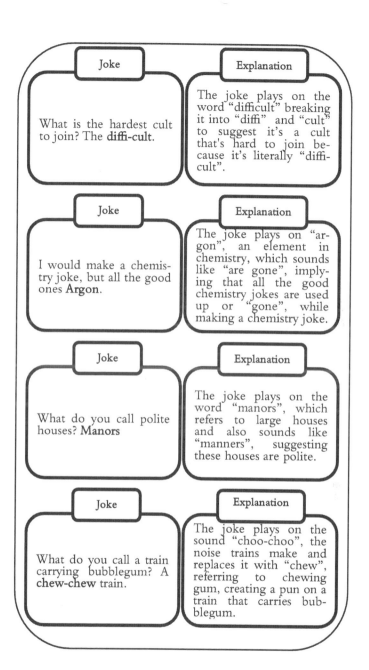

Joke	Explanation
Did you hear about the man who only collected rare pennies? He did not have a lot of **common cents**.	The joke plays on "common cents", referring both to common sense (practical judgment) and common pennies (ordinary coins), suggesting the man lacks both.
I accidentally sprayed deodorant into my mouth. Now when I talk I have this weird **Axe scent**.	The joke plays on "Axe scent", referring to Axe, the deodorant brand and sounding like "accent", suggesting the speaker now has a strange "accent" after spraying Axe in their mouth.
Why did the bicycle fall over? Because it was **two-tired**.	The joke plays on "two-tired", which sounds like "too tired" (exhausted) and refers to the bicycle's two tires, which make it impossible to stand on its own.
What did the pirate say when he turned 80? **Aye matey**.	The joke plays on "Aye matey", a typical pirate phrase, which sounds like "I'm eighty", humorously implying the pirate is announcing his age.

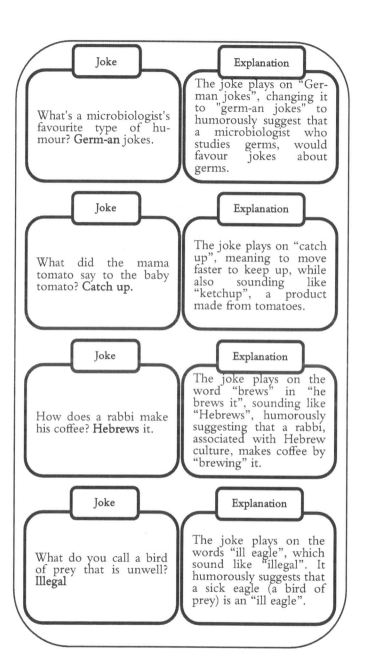

Joke	Explanation
Why couldn't the bad sailor learn the alphabet? Because he always got lost at "C"	The joke plays on the word "C", which sounds like "sea", suggesting that the sailor always got lost at sea, preventing him from learning the alphabet.
Why did the frog take the bus to work today? His car got **toad** away.	The joke plays on the word "toad", a type of amphibian related to frogs, which sounds like "towed" (when a car is taken away).
What do you call an angry counseller? A **therapissed**.	The joke plays on the word "therapist", changing it to "ther-apissed", which sounds like a therapist who is angry ("pissed" being slang for angry), suggesting an upset counsellor.
What did the biologist wear to impress the chemistry professor? Designer **genes**.	The joke plays on "designer genes", which sounds like "designer jeans" suggesting that the biologist wore impressive genetic traits to impress the chemistry professor.

Situational jokes

Life is full of moments that, on the surface, might seem mundane - but these everyday situations are often ripe for laughter. Situational jokes capture those small but universally funny scenarios we all find ourselves in, from the awkward tension of a first date to the quiet panic of realizing you've been walking around with spinach in your teeth. These jokes aren't just about clever punchlines; they're about turning life's little challenges, misunderstandings and quirks into moments of shared amusement. They remind us that humour doesn't always need to be outrageous or exaggerated; sometimes, the funniest stories are the ones that could happen to anyone, anytime.

A classic example of situational humour is the joke: "What does a snail say on the back of a tortoise? ----- Hui Hui Hui Huiiiiiiiiiiiiiiiiii" - This joke plays on the contrast between the perceptions of speed (for a human, both snails and tortoises are slow animals), but the snail perceives the tortoise's relatively slow pace as fast, leading to the exaggerated "Hui Hui Hui Huiiiiiiiiiiiiiiiii" sound, mimicking someone going fast.

Situational humour has a unique power: it allows us to laugh at our own lives, softening the impact of awkward encounters and frustrating moments. Ever tried to impress someone only to embarrass yourself completely? Or had a well-intentioned comment misunderstood? These situations can make us cringe at the time, but with a little distance, they're funny precisely because they're so common. In the following sections, each joke will not only capture these recognizable moments but also include a brief explanation that breaks down the humour. This way, you can see exactly how each joke builds on a universal truth or plays with the expectations we all share. Whether it's the unwritten rule of school life or the chaos of travel, you'll get a clear view of how humour transforms everyday situations into comedy. So, get ready to see ordinary life in a new, hilarious light.

Joke	Explanation
My GPS just told me to turn around. Now I cannot see where I am driving.	The joke plays on the GPS instruction to "turn around", which typically means to change direction and go back the way you came. However, the humour arises from the literal interpretation that the driver has turned around themselves so they can no longer see where they are driving, suggesting a humorous consequence of following the GPS instructions too literally.
How many Brexiteers does it take to change a light bulb? One to promise a brighter future and the rest to screw it up.	The joke plays on the Brexiteers' promise of a "brighter future" after Brexit, with "screwing up" referring to both installing a light bulb (which involves screwing it in) and the perceived complications and mistakes associated with Brexit, humorously suggesting that the outcome is far from the promised improvement.

Joke	Explanation
I do not mean to brag, but yesterday I beat our local chess champion in less than five moves. Finally I was able to put my high-school karate lessons to some	The joke starts as though the speaker won a chess game impressively quickly, suggesting they're skilled at chess. But the punchline twists the expectation by revealing that instead of actually playing chess, they used karate from high school to "beat" the champion physically, not through skill or strategy, making it a funny misunderstanding of the phrase "beating" someone in chess.
People often say that most women want to get married but I do not think that's true! I have asked many and they have all said no.	The joke plays on the idea that "most women want to get married", but here, the speaker humorously twists it by revealing that every woman they've proposed to has said "no", suggesting that maybe women don't want to marry him specifically, rather than challenging the general stereotype.

Joke	Explanation
Why are elephants wrinkly? Because you cannot iron them.	The joke points out that elephants are naturally wrinkly and then gives a silly, unexpected reason: they're wrinkly because they can't be ironed, as if they were a piece of clothing. This creates humour by applying a household task (ironing) to an elephant, a large animal you would never realistically iron, making the explanation both funny and absurd.
Hear about the new restaurant called Karma? There is no menu. You get what you deserve.	The joke plays on the concept of karma, where people get outcomes based on their past actions. At the fictional "Karma" restaurant, there's no menu because you get what you "deserve", humorously suggesting your meal depends on your own past behaviour instead of what you might want to order.

Joke

Why did the pothole apply for a job in road maintenance? Because it wanted to work from the inside to create chaos!

Explanation

The joke imagines a pothole as if it were a person applying for a road maintenance job. By "working from the inside", the pothole would cause even more road damage rather than fixing it.

Potholes are a hot topic in the UK. Many drivers and cyclists find potholes not only frustrating but also dangerous, and repairs are often delayed. The condition of roads are an ongoing topic in local and national discussions.

Joke

Some people these days are too judgmental. I can tell just by looking at them

Explanation

The joke is about judging others for being judgmental, which creates an ironic twist: the speaker criticizes people for being judgmental while admitting to doing the same thing by just looking at them. This funny contradiction points out how easy it is to fall into the behaviour we criticize in others.

Joke	Explanation
What did the left eye say to the right eye? Between you and me, something smells.	The joke is a play on words and anatomy. The left and right eyes are talking to each other, and "between" them is the nose, which smells, making it a humorous way for the eyes to point out that something literally "smells" between them.
My girlfriend told me that I am pretty. Well the whole sentence was, "You are pretty annoying", but I try to focus on the positive things.	The joke humorously shows selective hearing: the speaker's girlfriend actually called him "pretty annoying", but he chooses to focus only on the word "pretty", ignoring the rest of the sentence. This creates a funny contrast between the girlfriend's intended insult and the speaker's attempt to take it as a compliment.

Joke	Explanation
A priest, a rabbi, and a vicar walk into a bar. They get to talking and start arguing over who's the best at converting. One says: "I bet I could even convert a BEAR!" and they all agree to try. Next day, the priest says: "I sprinkled a bear with holy water and it started to pray!" The vicar says "I wrestled and baptized a bear! He became docile as a lamb!" The rabbi, covered in blood, mumbles: "Circumcision was not the best way to start."	The joke plays on the absurdity of religious leaders attempting to convert a bear, highlighting their competitive spirit. The priest and vicar boast about their impressive, yet improbable, feats of converting the bear through prayer and baptism. The punchline comes from the rabbi, who humorously reveals that his method was to perform circumcision on the bear, a clearly inappropriate and dangerous choice.

Joke	Explanation
A priest, a rabbi and a vicar walk into a bar. The barman says, "Is this some kind of joke?"	This joke relies on a classic setup where three characters from different religious backgrounds— a priest, a rabbi, and a vicar— enter a bar, which is often the beginning of various jokes. The punchline comes from the barman's response, "Is this some kind of joke?" This line flips the expectation because it acknowledges the setup itself as a joke.

Joke	Explanation
What do you call a Brit who gets impatient in a queue? An anomaly.	This joke plays on the stereotype that British people are very polite and always queue patiently. The punchline, "an anomaly", humorously suggests that a Brit who becomes impatient in a queue is such an unusual occurrence that they stand out as a rare exception. The humour comes from contrasting expected behaviour - patience in line - with the unexpected impatience, poking fun at the stereotype.
A fortune teller told me that in 12 years time, I would suffer terrible heartbreak. So I bought a puppy to cheer me up.	This joke revolves around a fortune teller predicting "terrible heartbreak" in 12 years. The punchline, "So I bought a puppy to cheer me up," is hinting to the fact that dogs typically have a life expectancy of around 12 years, hinting that the very choice made to avoid heartbreak could lead to it when the dog eventually passes away.

Joke	Explanation
A bear walks into a bar and says: "Give me a whiskey and........cola". " Why the big pause?" asks the bartender. The bear shrugs. "I am not sure, I was born with them".	The joke plays on the words "big pause", which sound like "big paws". When the bartender asks why the bear paused, it's interpreted as a question about the bear's large paws. The bear humorously responds as if the question is about his physical traits, saying he was born with them.
What did 0 say to 8? Nice belt!	The joke plays on the shapes of the numbers 0 and 8. The "8" looks like a "0" with a "belt" tightened around its middle, giving it two loops instead of one, so the "0" compliments the "8" on its "belt".

Joke

A friend asked me: "As a little boy, was your mom strict with you?" I said: "My mum was never a little boy".

Explanation

In this joke, the friend is asking if the speaker's mom was strict with him when he was a little boy. Instead of answering about her parenting style, the speaker humorously twists the meaning, responding as if the friend meant was your mom ever a little boy? By taking the question literally, he gives an unexpected answer that points out the absurdity, making it funny through this playful misunderstanding.

Joke

My granddad used to say: "If it wasn't for me, you would all be speaking German!" He was a lovely man, but a horrible language teacher. I don't know why the school hired him.

Explanation

The joke plays on the phrase "If it wasn't for me, you'd all be speaking German", which is often used by war veterans to mean they helped prevent German occupation. Here, however, the granddad was actually a bad language teacher who didn't teach German well at all.

Joke	Explanation
They say an Englishman laughs three times at a joke. The first time when everyone gets it, the second time when he thinks he gets it, and the third time when he realizes he doesn't.	The joke humorously suggests that an Englishman laughs at a joke in three stages: first, he laughs politely, then laughs again, believing he understands it; and finally, he laughs about himself, poking fun at the stereotype of English reserve and delayed understanding.
My wife asked for a divorce today, saying I was too un-british. I saw it coming from a kilometre away.	The joke is about the wife's complaint that her husband is "too un-British", but he proves her point with his response. He says he "saw it coming from a kilometre away", which uses the metric system, not the British-preferred imperial system (miles). This subtle difference shows how he actually is un-British in his choice of measurement, making the wife's complaint humorously accurate.

Joke

"If there are any idiots in the room, will they please stand up", said the sarcastic teacher. After a long silence, one student rose to his feet. "Now then mister, why do you consider yourself an idiot?", inquired the teacher. "Well, actually I don't", said the student, "but I hate to see you standing up there all by yourself".

Explanation

The joke begins with a sarcastic remark from the teacher, suggesting that anyone who feels like an idiot should stand up, expecting no one to comply. However, one student stands up, turning the situation around. When the teacher questions him, the student cleverly explains that he doesn't think he's an idiot; instead, he stands to keep the teacher company and therefore describes the teacher as an idiot.

Joke

I ordered a chicken and an egg from Amazon. I will let you know!

Explanation

This joke plays on the classic chicken-and-egg dilemma about which came first. The punchline is that the speaker ordered both from Amazon and humorously implies they're waiting to see which arrives first, creating a playful twist on the age-old question.

Joke	Explanation
When I moved into my new Igloo, my friends arranged a house warming party. Now I am homeless.	The joke plays on the term "housewarming party", which is a celebration held when someone moves into a new home. The punchline reveals a twist: the new home, which is made of ice and snow, melts during the celebrations due to the additional heat, leaving the person homeless.

Joke	Explanation
A guy said to God, "God, is it true that to you a billion years is like a second?" God said yes. The guy said, "God, is it true that to you a billion dollars is like a penny?" God said yes. The guy said, "God, can I have a penny?" God said, "Sure, just a second."	In the joke, a man asks God if a billion years feels like a second and if a billion dollars feels like a penny, to which God agrees. When the man then requests a penny, he's essentially asking for a billion dollars. God humorously confirmed the giving in a second, meaning a billion years, longer than the human lifespan.

Joke	Explanation
The inventor of Tupperware died. The funeral will take place once they can find the right lid for the coffin.	This joke plays on the well-known frustration with Tupperware lids: they're often hard to find or match correctly. The punchline imagines the same issue happening with the inventor's coffin, humorously suggesting that the funeral will be delayed until they can find a lid that fits.
My grandpa overdosed on viagra. They could not close the coffin.	This joke plays on the well-known effect of Viagra, which is used to treat erectile dysfunction. The punchline humorously suggests that after taking too much, the grandpa died and the effect was so strong that it caused the coffin to stay open. The humour lies in the exaggerated, absurd image of a coffin that can't be closed due to Viagra's effect on the middle section of the grandpa.

Joke	Explanation
My nagging wife died suddenly on a trip to Jerusalem. Funeral director: "Sir, it would cost about $45,000 if we send her home back to the states or $500 if we bury her here in Jerusalem." Me: "Ship her home." Funeral director: "But sir, why don't you bury her here in the Holy Land and you can save money." Me: "A long time ago a man was buried here and 3 days later he rose from the dead, I can't take that chance."	This joke is a classic example of dark British humour - a style known for its dry wit, irreverence, and often morbid themes. The setup plays on the common trope of a husband expressing frustration with a "nagging wife." The punchline then brings in a twist: the husband insists on the high-cost option of sending her home for burial because of the biblical reference to Jesus's resurrection after being buried in Jerusalem.
Why do golf commentators whisper? They do not want to wake up their audience.	This joke plays on the stereotype that golf can be slow and quiet, sometimes even dull, to the point where it might put viewers to sleep. Golf commentators typically whisper to avoid distracting the players, but here the joke suggests they whisper so softly because they don't want to disturb the sleeping audience.

Joke

A tough old cowboy from Texas counselled his granddaughter that if she wanted to live a long life, the secret was to sprinkle a pinch of gun powder on her oatmeal every morning. The granddaughter did this religiously until the age of 103, when she died. She left behind 14 children, 30 grandchildren, 45 great-grandchildren, 25 great-great-grandchildren, and a 40-foot hole where the crematorium used to be.

Explanation

This joke combines a cowboy's tough advice with a wild twist. The cowboy tells his granddaughter that adding gunpowder to her oatmeal will help her live a long life. She follows this odd advice until she reaches 103, leaving behind a large family. The punchline reveals that the gunpowder, accumulated over the years, caused an explosion during her cremation - a playful exaggeration of her commitment to his unconventional advice.

Joke

They say childbirth is the most painful experience, but I am not sure. Maybe I was too young to remember, but I do not think it hurt that much.

Explanation

This joke plays on the misunderstanding of childbirth pain. It's widely said that childbirth is one of the most painful experiences, but here, the speaker humorously twists it by pretending to interpret it as their own birth, suggesting they don't remember it hurting. While obviously no one can remember their own birth.

Joke

A guy asks a lawyer about his fees." I charge $50 for three questions", the lawyer says. "That's awfully steep, isn't it?", the guy asks. "Yes, I suppose so", the lawyer replies. "Now what's your final question?"

Explanation

In this joke, a guy is inquiring about a lawyer's fees, which are $50 for three questions. When the guy comments that this price is "awfully steep" he unknowingly uses up the second of his three questions, with the first one having been the question for the price. The humour develops when the lawyer agrees to the comment about the high price, but also strictly notes, that any question counts. The joke is showcasing a playful critique of legal fees.

Joke

Why do British politicians make great stand-up comedians? Because they've had plenty of practice delivering jokes in the House of Commons!

Explanation

This joke plays on the idea that British politicians often engage in lively, witty or sometimes absurd debates in the House of Commons. By saying they've "had plenty of practice delivering jokes," it humorously suggests that their speeches and arguments can be so ridiculous or laughable that they seem more like stand-up comedy than serious politicians.

Joke

Why did the conjoined twins move to England? So the other one could drive.

Explanation

This joke plays on the concept of conjoined twins, who are physically connected and share some body parts. The joke suggests that in other parts of Europe, only one of the conjoined twins could drive, leading them to move to England so that the other twin can take a break while the other one drives. The joke implies that the twins can only find a solution to their driving situation by relocating, which is inherently absurd.

Joke

"I'm on a whiskey diet. I've lost three days already."

Explanation

This joke plays on the idea of a "diet", which typically refers to a regimen for losing weight, but the punchline humorously suggests that the speaker has lost track of time instead of weight due to drinking whiskey. The phrase "I've lost three days already" implies that excessive drinking has made them forget those days, highlighting the absurdity of claiming to be on a diet while indulging in alcohol.

Joke	Explanation
What do you call a thief who keeps the things he stole on public display? British.	This joke is a reference to famous British museums, especially the British Museum, which has numerous artifacts and treasures from around the world that were acquired during colonial times. The joke implies that these items are "stolen" yet kept on public display, making the "thief" in the joke "British."
People call me self-centred. But that is enough about them.	The humour here comes from the contradiction in what the speaker says versus what they do. They start by acknowledging that people think they're self-centred, but then immediately dismiss everyone else to keep the focus on themselves. This response ironically proves the claim of being self-centred without them realizing it.

Joke	Explanation
A man goes to a doctor and says, "Doctor, I have a serious problem. I can never remember anything." The doctor says, "That's very serious indeed. How long have you had this problem?" The man says, "What problem?"	This joke plays on the idea that the man's memory problem is so severe that he instantly forgets things - even moments after they're discussed. When the doctor asks how long he's had the issue, the man's response, "What problem?" reveals he's already forgotten the conversation about his own memory loss, highlighting the extent of his forgetfulness in a funny, exaggerated way.

Joke	Explanation
What workout plan did Jesus have? Crossfit	This joke is a play on words, using "CrossFit", a popular high-intensity workout program, and "cross", referring to the crucifixion of Jesus. The humour lies in linking Jesus's association with the cross to the modern workout style, as if he had his own version of "CrossFit".

Joke	Explanation
A mate of mine named his dog "Ten Miles", so he told everyone he regularly walked ten miles. But today, he ran over Ten Miles.	This joke is a play on the dual meaning of "Ten Miles," both as the name of the friend's dog and as a literal distance. The humour kicks in at the end, where "he ran over Ten Miles" sounds like he covered a distance, but it actually means he accidentally hit his dog, Ten Miles, with his car.
The inventor of the USB port died. They started to lower his coffin into the grave, and then they raised it up, turned it around, and put it in the right way. Then raised it again, turned it back around, and somehow it fit that way the second time.	This joke plays on the famously tricky nature of USB ports: they often seem impossible to insert correctly on the first try, requiring you to flip them, sometimes multiple times, to get them to fit. In this joke, the USB inventor's funeral mirrors that same frustrating back-and-forth of inserting a USB, humorously suggesting that even his coffin had to be repeatedly repositioned before finally fitting properly.

Joke	Explanation
How many Brits does it take to change a lightbulb? None, they'd rather sit in the dark and grumble about it.	This joke plays on the stereotype that Brits are stoic and often prefer to complain rather than take action. Instead of changing the light bulb, they'd rather sit in the dark, quietly grumbling about the inconvenience. It humorously exaggerates British reluctance to fix problems directly, poking fun at a dry, reserved attitude toward small annoyances.
What is the longest word in the English language? Smiles. The first and last letter are a mile apart.	This joke plays with the word "smiles" by using a literal interpretation of "a mile apart". The setup suggests "smiles" is long due to the distance between its first and last letters, "s" and "s". Since the word contains the letters "mile" in between, it cleverly uses this imagery to make a joke about the word's "length".

Joke	Explanation
What do you call a beautiful woman in England? A tourist.	This joke pokes fun at the stereotype that British beauty standards or fashion are less glamorous compared to other places, implying that the "beautiful" woman must be a visitor rather than a local.
A detective showed up at my house and asked me where I was between seven and eight. I told him I was at school.	This joke plays with the double meaning of "between seven and eight." The detective means between 7:00 and 8:00 (as in time), but the person humorously interprets it as between ages seven and eight, giving the alibi that they were at school at that age. The joke twists an expected question into a playful misunderstanding about time and age.

Joke	Explanation
How will British Christmas dinners be different after Brexit? No Brussels.	This joke plays on the double meaning of "Brussels" to poke fun at the changes Brexit might bring to British traditions. Traditionally, British Christmas dinners often include Brussels sprouts. But after Brexit, the joke suggests there will be "no Brussels" — referring both to the vegetable and to Brussels, the capital of the EU, highlighting Britain's separation from Europe.

Joke	Explanation
A cruise ship passes by a remote island, and all the passengers see a bearded man running around and waving his arms wildly. "Captain," one passenger asks, "who is that man over there?" "I have no idea," the captain says, "but he goes nuts every year when we pass him."	This joke is about a stranded man on a remote island, desperate for help. Every time the cruise ship passes, he waves frantically, hoping to be rescued. But the captain and passengers misunderstand, thinking he's just excited to see them rather than recognizing he's stranded and in need of help. So instead of stopping, they keep sailing on, leaving him there.

Joke	Explanation
My wife asked me to prepare our son for school. So I stole his lunch.	The wife's request to "prepare" their son for school was likely intended as helping him get ready, like making his lunch, packing his backpack or making sure he's dressed. Instead, the husband "prepares" their son by doing something completely unexpected by taking his lunch, as though the lesson is that life isn't always fair. It's a funny twist on what it means to get "prepared".
A woman gets on a bus with her baby. The bus driver says, "That's the ugliest baby I've ever seen." The woman is furious and walks to the back of the bus. She sits next to a man and says, "The driver just insulted my baby." The man says, "That's outrageous. You should go back and give him a piece of your mind. Here, I'll hold your monkey for you."	This joke relies on two unexpected insults. First, the bus driver rudely calls the woman's baby "ugly". Upset, she sits beside a man who suggests she confront the driver, implying he's on her side. But, in a twist, he calls the baby a "monkey" while offering to hold it, adding to the insult. The humour comes from the man's failed attempt to be supportive, which only makes things worse.

Joke

A guy is sitting at home when he hears a knock at the door. He opens the door and sees a snail on the porch. He picks up the snail and throws it as far as he can. A year later, there's another knock at the door. He opens it and sees the same snail. The snail says, "What was that all about?"

Explanation

In this joke, the humour comes from the contrast of the man's hasty action and the snail's incredibly slow nature. A year after the snail was thrown, the snail returns, and is still upset and asks, "What was that all about?" This punchline plays on the absurdity of a snail taking such a long time to reach the same spot, highlighting its slow speed and creating a humourous scenario where the snail is unfazed by the year-long journey.

Joke

I told my wife she should embrace her mistakes. She gave me a hug.

Explanation

This joke is a play on words and self-deprecation. When the husband says his wife should "embrace her mistakes", he means she should accept and learn from things she's done wrong. But the punchline is that she takes it literally and hugs him, implying he is one of her mistakes. It's that unexpected twist that brings the humour.

Joke

I'm writing a paper on the benefits of procrastination. I'll start it tomorrow.

Explanation

The humour comes from the irony of planning to write about the benefits of procrastination but then delaying it. It pokes fun at the tendency to put things off, even when acknowledging the habit itself.

Joke

During my check-up I asked the Doctor, "Do you think I'll live a long and healthy life then?" He replied, "I doubt it somehow. Mercury is in Uranus right now". I said, "I don't go in for any of that astrology nonsense". He replied, "Neither do I. My thermometer just broke".

Explanation

This joke combines medical humour with a play on words involving astrology. Initially, the patient asks the doctor about his health, but the doctor's response is unexpected: he mentions "Mercury is in Uranus", a phrase associated with astrology. The punchline reveals the doctor's actual concern: his thermometer has broken, implying that toxic Mercury, which was used in thermometers, is now inside the patient.

Joke

What's a British person's idea of a spicy meal? A curry with a hint of black pepper.

Explanation

The joke is a playful nod to the stereotype that British cuisine is generally mild in comparison to the more flavourful and spicy cuisines from around the world. The joke exaggerates this by suggesting that just a hint of black pepper is enough to be considered spicy. It highlights the cultural differences in food preferences in a cheeky way.

Joke

A man is walking through the woods when he sees a bear charging at him. He runs away, but he knows he can't outrun a bear for long, so he starts praying, "Dear Lord, I beg you. Please, o Lord, please let this bear be a Christian!" The bear catches up to him, knocks him down on the ground, then gets on its knees and says, "Dear Lord, thank you for this food I am about to receive..."

Explanation

This joke hinges on a twist involving expectations versus reality. The man prays for the bear to be Christian, hoping it means the bear will show mercy. Instead, the bear's version of being Christian is praying before eating its meal - and the meal is the man. The unexpected punchline catches you off guard, making it funny in a dark way.

Joke

I bought coconut shampoo today. But when I got home, I realised I do not even have a coconut.

Explanation

The humour stems from the absurdity of buying a product named "coconut sham-poo" and then stating that without an actual coconut, the product would be pointless. It exaggerates the misunderstanding for comedic effect, highlighting the absurdity of taking product names too literally.

Joke

A man walks down a street and sees a boy jumping on a box. The boy shouts "16, 16,16, 16,....". The man is wondering and asks: "Why are you jumping on the box and scream 16?". The boy answers: "it's so much fun! You should try it!". The man hesitates but then steps on the box and jumps. The boy pulls away the box and the man falls through a manhole. The boy puts the box back on, gets back up on the box and shouts: "17,17, 17, 17...."

Explanation

This joke uses situational irony and a touch of dark humour. The boy's chant of "16" suggests something intriguing, and the man's curiosity gets the better of him. When the boy encourages the man to join, the unexpected twist is that it's a setup, leading to the man's fall through the manhole. The punchline is the boy continuing to count up to "17", implying he's been tricking others and keeps a tally of his victims.

Joke

I'm writing a book on reverse psychology. Do not read it!

Explanation

This joke is clever because it plays on the concept of reverse psychology, where telling someone not to do something often makes them want to do it even more. By saying "Do not read it!" the author is ironically encouraging readers to pick up the book out of curiosity. The humour comes from the contradiction between the instruction and the likely reaction it will provoke.

Joke

It is our wedding anniversary soon and my wife is leaving jewellery catalogues everywhere. I got the hint! I bought her a magazine rack.

Explanation

This joke plays on the idea of misunderstanding hints. The husband's wife is dropping hints about wanting jewellery for their anniversary by leaving catalogues around, implying she wants him to buy her some jewellery. However, instead of taking the hint, he misinterprets it and buys her a magazine rack, which is practical but misses the romantic intent altogether.

Joke	Explanation
Last night I was laying in bed and looked at the stars and was thinking: Wait, where is my roof?	The humour arises from the sudden shift in focus from admiring the beauty of the stars to the practical concern of not having a roof over one's head. It's funny because it contrasts a romantic moment of contemplation with the absurdity of being caught off guard by a lack of shelter, suggesting a whimsical naivety about one's living situation.
If you think your job is tough, remember there's someone out there whose job is to install turn signals in BMWs.	This joke uses irony to highlight the stereotype of BMW drivers as reckless or inconsiderate on the road. The humour lies in the implication that turn signals are often not used by BMW drivers, making the job of installing them seem pointless. It suggests that the installer has a tough job because they're putting in turn signals that will likely go unused.

Joke	Explanation
My boss was honest with me today. He pulled up to work with his sweet new car this morning and I complimented him on it. He replied, "Well, if you work hard, set goals, stay determined and put in long hours, I can get an even better one next year".	This joke plays on the boss's unexpected twist in response to the compliment. The speaker initially thinks the boss will share a motivational story about working hard to achieve personal success. Instead, the boss implies that all the employee's hard work and dedication will mainly benefit him, not the employee. The punchline reveals the irony of corporate work culture: despite employees' hard work, it's often the higher-ups who reap the rewards.
What's the difference between a boyfriend and a husband? About 30 pounds.	This joke highlights the stereotypical idea that people often gain weight after getting married, especially men. The punchline implies that as a boyfriend becomes a husband, he might gradually put on some extra pounds due to feeling more settled and relaxed in the relationship, no longer needing to impress as much.

Joke

For a high school dance, the head boy asked out the girl he liked. To get flowers for her, he had to stand in a line outside the florist for an hour. To make things worse, he had to wait another hour in a line outside the tuxedo shop. Finally, he goes to the dance with the girl. The girl wanted to have some apple punch, so the boy went to get it, but to his surprise, there was no punch line.

Explanation

This joke's humour lies in its play on the phrase "punch line". It sets up a narrative involving various lines the boy stands in: at the florist, at the tuxedo shop, and finally, he goes to get punch at the dance. The twist is that the expected "punch line" is missing, both literally (there's no line to get punch) and figuratively (the joke ends without a traditional punchline).

Joke

What do you call a gorilla with a banana in each ear? Anything you want, it can't hear you!

Explanation

This joke is a playful mix of literal and absurd humour. It asks a silly question with an equally silly setup: a gorilla with bananas in its ears. The punchline cleverly flips the expectation by highlighting the absurdity - the gorilla can't hear you because its ears are blocked. So, you can call it anything you want.

Joke	Explanation
If anyone is alone this Christmas and has nobody to spend it with, please let me know. I really need to borrow some chairs.	This joke cleverly combines (missing) empathy and humour. It starts off sounding like a heartfelt invitation to help those who might be lonely during Christmas, but twists unexpectedly into a request to borrow chairs. The humour lies in the sudden shift from a seemingly caring message to a practical need, playing on the reader's expectations.
Do you know why you never see an elephant hiding in a tree? Because they are really good at it. Do you know why elephants paint their balls red? So, they can hide in cherry trees. Do you know what the loudest noise is in the jungle? A giraffe eating cherries.	This joke relies on absurdity and unexpected twists. It starts with a classic riddle format, suggesting elephants are great at hiding in trees, which is absurd given their size. The second part claims elephants paint their balls red to blend in with cherry trees. The final line delivers the punchline, by introducing a giraffe making noise while eating cherries, which would have been the elephant's balls.

Joke

How is Christmas exactly like your job? You do all the work and some fat guy in a suit gets all the credit.

Explanation

This joke draws a parallel between the effort one puts into their job and the familiar dynamics of Christmas. It suggests that much like in many workplaces where the employee does the bulk of the labour but the boss receive recognition, during Christmas, the hard work of gift-giving, decorating, and preparing often goes unnoticed while Santa Claus gets all the credit for delivering presents and spreading joy.

Joke

If trump wins the election: I will leave the United States!
If Biden wins the election, I will leave the United States!
This is not a political joke, I just want to travel.

Explanation

This joke humorously highlights the extreme reactions some people have to presidential elections in the United States. However, the punchline reveals that the motivation isn't a deep political sentiment but rather a desire to travel, poking fun at the exaggerated claims often made during election seasons.

Joke	Explanation
A taxi passenger tapped the driver on the shoulder to ask him a question. The driver screamed, lost control of the car, nearly hit a bus, went up on the footpath, and stopped inches from a shop window. For a second, everything was quiet in the cab. Then the driver said, "Look, mate, don't ever do that again. You scared the living daylights out of me!" The passenger apologized and said, "I didn't realize that a little tap would scare you so much". The driver replied, "Sorry, it's not really your fault. Today is my first day as a cab driver — I've been driving a funeral van for the last 25 years."	In this joke, the taxi driver reacts dramatically to a simple tap on the shoulder, causing a chaotic, near-disastrous scene. Afterwards, he explains that he used to drive a funeral van for 25 years—a vehicle that obviously transports the deceased, so he's not used to any unexpected movements or sounds from his passengers! This background gives his overreaction a funny twist, as he instinctively panics when he feels a tap, conditioned by years of driving passengers who, well, don't tap.

Joke	Explanation
Four men are in the hospital waiting room because their wives are having babies. A nurse goes up to the first guy and says, "Congratulations! You're the father of twins." "That's odd", answers the man. "I work for the Minnesota Twins!" A nurse says to the second guy, "Congratulations! You're the father of triplets!" "That's weird," answers the second man. "I work for the 3M company!" A nurse tells the third man, "Congratulations! You're the father of quadruplets!" "That's strange," he answers. "I work for the Four Seasons hotel!" The last man is groaning and banging his head against the wall. "What's wrong?" the others ask. "I work for 7 Up!"	In this joke, each man's job seems to predict the number of babies their wives are having. The first man, who works for the "Minnesota Twins", has twins, the second man from "3M" has triplets, and the third from "Four Seasons" has quadruplets. The punchline is the fourth man, who is horrified because he works for "7 Up" - implying he's worried he'll be the father of seven! The joke plays on the coincidence between each man's employer and the number of babies, making the final twist both funny and absurdly worrisome for the last man.

Joke

It's the World Cup Final, and a man makes his way to his seat right next to the pitch. He sits down, noticing that the seat next to him is empty. He leans over and asks his neighbour if someone will be sitting there. "No," says the neighbour. "The seat is empty." "This is incredible," said the man. "Who in their right mind would have a seat like this for the Final and not use it?" The neighbour says, "Well actually the seat belongs to me. I was supposed to come with my wife, but she passed away. This is the first World Cup Final we haven't been to together since we got married." "Oh, I'm so sorry to hear that. That's terrible....But couldn't you find someone else, a friend, relative or even a neighbour to take her seat?" The man shakes his head. "No", he says. "They're all at her funeral."

Explanation

In this joke, the man at the World Cup Final has an empty seat next to him, which belonged to his late wife. While this seems heartfelt at first, the punchline reveals that instead of attending her funeral, he chose to honour their tradition of attending the World Cup Final. The humour comes from the absurdity and dark irony that he prioritized the game over paying final respects, showing a humorous (if exaggerated) take on how dedicated some people are to their sports traditions.

Knock-knock jokes

British humour is celebrated worldwide for its wit, wordplay and often dry or absurd sense of humour. Within this landscape, knock-knock jokes hold a unique position, cherished for their simplicity and potential for clever wordplay. They are primarily child's jokes and are as much a part of British humour as classic sitcoms and stand-up routines. This chapter explores the origins of knock-knock jokes, their special connection to British humour and share a few examples.

The roots of knock-knock jokes can be traced back to the call-and-response structure found in traditional stage performances. This format, where one person says something and another responds, has been a part of storytelling for centuries. Shakespeare himself utilized a similar structure in "Macbeth". In the play, a porter humorously interacts with imaginary visitors knocking at the gate. This scene is often considered one of the earliest known examples of knock-knock joke structure. The modern knock-knock joke as we know it began to take shape in the 20th century, particularly during the vaudeville era in the US, where quick, witty exchanges were a hit with audiences. The simple, repetitive format made them easy to remember and share, contributing to their popularity.

By the mid-20th century, knock-knock jokes had cemented their place in popular culture. They became a favourite among children and adults alike, thanks to their easy setup and the anticipation built by the "Who's there?"

and subsequent responses. Knock-knock jokes endure because they are universally accessible. They play on language and expectations in a way that transcends age and background. Their simplicity allows for endless variations, keeping them fresh and engaging. Despite their often predictable format, they have a charm that keeps people coming back for more.

Knock-knock jokes follow a simple, yet engaging structure:

- Initiation: One person says "Knock, knock."
- Response: The other person responds with "Who's there?"
- Setup: The first person gives a name or phrase, often a wordplay or homophones. For example, "Lettuce."
- Question: The second person replies with the name or phrase followed by "who?" e.g., "Lettuce who?"
- Punchline: The first person delivers the punchline, which is usually a play on words: "Lettuce in, it's cold out here!"

In knock-knock jokes, wordplay usually involves puns or homophones - words that sound alike but have different meanings. Here's a further breakdown of the knock-knock joke structure, excluding the always similar introduction of "Knock Knock" and "Who is there?":

Setup with ambiguity: The following phrase or name given by the joker is ambiguous or has a double meaning. Example: "Lettuce" sounds like "Let us."

Question for clarity: The respondent's "who?" clarifies the setup phrase, leading to a rephrased version that brings out the pun. Example: "Lettuce who?" sounds like "Let us who?"

Punchline revelation: The punchline capitalizes on the double meaning, delivering a clever twist or humorous outcome. Example: "Lettuce in, it's cold out here!" plays on the phrase "Let us in."

The beauty of knock-knock jokes lies in their simplicity and the playful use of language, making the punchline both unexpected and amusing. In the following we will look at some examples and the explanation will highlight the wordplay.

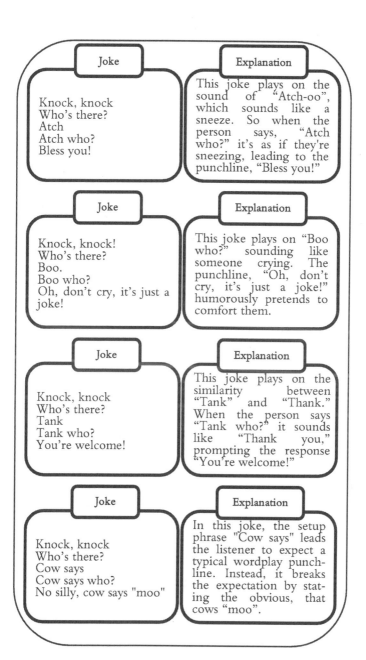

Joke

Knock, knock
Who's there?
Woo
Woo who?
Don't get too excited; it's just a knock-knock joke

Explanation

This joke plays on the natural reaction to "Woo" sounding like "Woo-hoo!" - an expression of excitement.

Joke

Knock, knock
Who's there?
Alpaca
Alpaca who?
Alpaca the suitcase, you load up the car

Explanation

This joke uses a fun pun on "Alpaca", making it sound like "I'll pack a." The punchline, "Alpaca the suitcase, you load up the car", cleverly combines the name with an action.

Joke

Knock, knock
Who's there?
Europe
Europe who?
No, you're a poo!

Explanation

This joke is a play on words with the phrase "Europe who", which, when spoken out loud, sounds like "You're a poo."

Joke

Knock, knock
Who's there?
Hawaii
Hawaii who?
I'm good, Hawaii you?

Explanation

This joke is a playful use of word sounds to mimic a greeting. When you say, "Hawaii who?" it sounds like, "How are you?" - so the reply, is "I'm good, Hawaii you?"

Joke	Explanation
Knock, knock Who's there? Luke Luke who? Luke through the peep-hole and find out!	This joke plays on the name "Luke", which sounds like "look." The punchline suggests the listener should "look" through the peep-hole to find out who's there.
Knock, knock Who's there? Robin Robin who? Robin you! Hand over your cash!	This joke uses the name "Robin", which sounds like "robbin." The punchline is suggesting that the person at the door is actually a robber demanding cash.
Knock, knock Who's there? Harry Harry who? Harry up, it's cold out here!	his joke uses the name "Harry", which sounds like "hurry." The punchline turns it into a demand to speed things up because it's cold outside.
Knock, knock Who's there? Beets Beets who? Beets me!	This joke plays on the phrase "Beats me", which means "I don't know." By using "Beets", a vegetable, instead, it creates a pun.

Joke	Explanation
Knock, knock Who's there? Lettuce Lettuce who? Lettuce entertain you!	This joke uses "Lettuce" to sound like "Let us." The punchline cleverly turns it into an invitation: "Lettuce entertain you!"
Knock, knock Who's there? Bee Bee who? Bee-lieve me, these jokes get better!	The joke plays on the sound of "bee" and "be". The word "Bee" leads to a pun with the phrase "Believe me, these jokes get better". Hint: They won't be getting better...
Knock, knock Who's there? Ice cream Ice cream who? Ice cream every time I see a scary movie!	This knock-knock joke plays on "Ice cream", which sounds like "I scream". The punchline reveals that the speaker "ice creams" (screams) every time they see a scary movie.
Knock, knock Who's there? To To who? No, no, it's to whom.	This joke is a clever twist on grammar correction. The setup leads the listener to respond with "To who?" and the punchline humorously corrects the grammar: "No, no, it's 'to whom."

Joke	Explanation
Knock, knock Who's there? Butter Butter who? Butter open up or I'll tell another joke!	This one uses "Butter" to sound like "Better", creating a playful twist in the punchline: "Butter open up or I'll tell another joke!"
Knock, knock Who's there? Owl Owl who? Yes, they do!	The joke uses "Owl who?" which sounds like "Owls hoo?" leading to the punchline "Yes, they do!" referencing that owls indeed "hoo".
Knock Knock who is there cargo cargo who, No, man. Owls go who. Car go beep beep.	The joke leads to think "cargo" is part of a regular phrase. Instead, the punchline points out the sound differences between animals and objects: "Owls go hooo. Car go beep beep."
Did you hear about the guy who invented the knock knock joke? He won the no-bell prize.	This joke plays on the pun between "Nobel Prize" and "no-bell". The inventor of the knock-knock joke receives a "no-bell" prize as he always knocks, instead of ringing.

Riddles

As we reach the close of this exploration of British humour, I hope it has given you a hearty laugh, an occasional "aha" moment and a window into the quirks and witticisms that make British humour so unique. From wordplay and puns to irony and understatement, we've journeyed through a comedy landscape that delights in the subtle, the dry and the downright cheeky.

British humour isn't merely about getting the punchline - it's about pausing to appreciate the twist, to catch the irony and sometimes to chuckle at the absurdity of everyday life. For some, it's an acquired taste; for others, it's an instant spark. Whatever your take, we hope this collection has helped you appreciate this distinctly British brand of comedy and that you found plenty of enjoyment along the way.

Now, as a fitting send-off, I leave you with a final section filled with classic riddles - no explanations, no hints. Just pure, unadulterated brain-teasers for you to mull over. Test your wit, share them with friends or just enjoy the little jokes. After all, sometimes the joy of humour lies not in the answer itself but in the fun of getting there.

Happy riddling and may the laughs continue long after you've turned the final page!

What falls but never needs a bandage?
The rain.

What's the leading cause of dry skin?
Towels.

Why did the golfer bring two pairs of pants?
In case he got a hole in one.

Why don't dogs make good dancers?
Because they have two left feet!

What did the ocean say to the beach?
Nothing, it just waved.

What's a German's favourite line in a book?
The deadline.

Which month is the shortest in the year?
May, it only has three letters.

What do you call it when a snowman throws a tantrum?
A meltdown.

Which is faster hot or cold?
Hot, because you can catch cold.

Where do fish sleep?
In the riverbed.

What do you call an alligator in the police force?
An investigator.

What do you call a bee that cant make up its mind?
Maybee.

What do you call a cow with no legs?
Ground beef.

What is Dumbledors hair stylist called?
Hairy Cutter.

What kind of drugs do the seven dwarves deal? Snow white.

What do you call a fish with no eyes?
Fsh.

What do you call a deer with no eyes?
No idea (eye dear).

What do you call a deer with no eyes and no legs? Still no idea (eye dear).

Acknowledgment

There are many names to be put down here, that made my time in the UK an experience of growing up, becoming independent and learning to appreciate new cultures, especially the British culture. A big thanks to all the people who welcomed a stranger in their country and made me feel at home. Thank you to everyone who took the time to share their rich culture, beautiful country and especially the British humour.

A special thank you to everyone who supported the writing and design of this book and my parents for always supporting all of my decisions.

Made in the USA
Columbia, SC
29 December 2024